Integrating Instruction

in

Math

Strategies, Activities, Projects, Tools, and Techniques

by Imogene Forte and Sandra Schurr

Incentive Publications, Inc.
Nashville, Tennessee

Illustrated by Marta Drayton
Cover by Geoffrey Brittingham
Edited by Jan Keeling

ISBN 0-86530-322-3

PRINTED IN THE UNITED STATES OF AMERICA

TABLE OF CONTENTS

Using Integrated Instructional Strategies to Accommodate Differing Learning Styles, Abilities, and Interests

Using Multiple Intelligences as an Instructional Tool

Using Learning Stations as an Instructional Tool

Using the Read and Relate Concept as an Instructional Tool

Using Integrated Instructional Strategies to Develop Problem-solving and Higher-order Thinking Skills

Using Bloom's Taxonomy as an Instructional Tool

Using Williams' Taxonomy as an Instructional Tool

Using Investigation Cards as an Instructional Tool

Using Calendars as an Instructional Tool

Using Integrated Instructional Strategies to Promote Cooperative Learning and Group Interaction

Using Integrated Instructional Strategies to Facilitate Authentic Assessment

A Very Practical Appendix

Preface

Middle grades educators are meeting the challenges of student-centered education with new teaching methods to create a positive learning climate for students in early adolescence. Middle grades math educators want to know how to use these new instructional strategies and organizational procedures in ways that are specifically designed for math classes.

Integrating Instruction in Math was created especially for math educators at the middle grade level. The high-interest activities cover topics in important areas in mathematics, including:

- Applied Mathematics
- General Mathematics
- Statistics/Probability
- Graphing
- Geometry
- Measurement
- Tessellations
- Computers
- Famous Mathematicians
- Careers in Math

In each of five major sections you will find a comprehensive overview of a particular instructional focus accompanied by stimulating activities that are meant to be used as well as to serve as examples.

USING INTEGRATED INSTRUCTIONAL STRATEGIES TO ACCOMMODATE DIFFERING LEARNING STYLES, ABILITIES, AND INTERESTS features guidelines for incorporating the Multiple Intelligences, Learning Stations, and Read and Relate tasks into the preparation of high-quality lesson plans and student assignments.

USING INTEGRATED INSTRUCTIONAL STRATEGIES TO DEVELOP PROBLEM-SOLVING AND HIGHER-ORDER THINKING SKILLS offers guidelines for infusing higher-order thinking skills into the educational process through the use of cognitive taxonomies, self-directed investigation cards, and calendars. The cognitive taxonomies offer useful foundations for the design of interdisciplinary units, student worksheets, learning stations, and group projects.

USING INSTRUCTIONAL STRATEGIES TO PROMOTE COOPERATIVE LEARNING AND GROUP INTERACTION presents valuable collaborative processes such as Think/Pair/Share, Three-step Interview, Circle of Knowledge, Team Learning, Round Table, and Jigsaw.

USING INTEGRATED INSTRUCTIONAL STRATEGIES TO FACILITATE AUTHENTIC ASSESSMENT shows how to effectively implement product, performance, and portfolio assessment practices. Included is a complete sample portfolio based on an interdisciplinary unit in mathematics.

Finally, **A VERY PRACTICAL APPENDIX** provides high-interest strategies and activities to integrate social studies, science, and language arts into the math curriculum; topics for student reports and journal writing; blank planning outlines to help in the creation of original lesson plans; and an annotated bibliography. A comprehensive index will make it easy to keep track of this wealth of information.

In short, this book is a must for all math educators, for those on interdisciplinary teams as well as those in self-contained classrooms. It offers a collection of instructional strategies that were designed for heterogeneous groups of students in an educational setting that will allow every student to be successful. It clarifies theoretical principles and offers activities that cover a wide range of important topics in math. Best of all, its content is fresh, original, and of interest to contemporary middle grades students.

Using Integrated Instructional Strategies to Accommodate Differing Learning Styles, Abilities, and Interests

Using Multiple Intelligences
as an Instructional Tool

Howard Gardner's Theory of the Multiple Intelligences provides teachers with an excellent model for the design of interdisciplinary units, student worksheets, learning stations, and group projects. Gardner is quick to point out that (1) every student has at least one dominant intelligence (although he or she may have more than one); (2) these intelligences can all be nurtured, strengthened, and taught over time; (3) the intelligences do not exist in isolation but interface and interact with one another when a student is completing a task; and (4) the intelligences provide teachers with seven different ways to approach the curriculum. Gardner has identified and described seven major intelligences:

VERBAL/LINGUISTIC DOMINANCE
Students strong in this type of intelligence have highly developed verbal skills, and often think in words. They do well on written assignments, enjoy reading, and are good at communicating and expressing themselves.

LOGICAL/MATHEMATICAL DOMINANCE
Students strong in this intelligence think in abstractions and handle complex concepts, and they readily see patterns or relationships in ideas. They like to work with numbers and perform mathematical operations, and approach problem-solving exercises with logic and rational thought.

VISUAL/SPATIAL DOMINANCE
Students with visual/spatial strength think in images, symbols, colors, pictures, patterns, and shapes. They like to perform tasks that require "seeing with the mind's eye"—tasks that require them to visualize, imagine, pretend, or form images.

BODY/KINESTHETIC DOMINANCE
Students dominant in this intelligence have a strong body awareness and a sharp sense of physical movement. They communicate best through body language, physical gestures, hands-on activities, active demonstrations, and performance tasks.

MUSICAL/RHYTHMIC DOMINANCE
Students with this dominant intelligence enjoy music, rhythmic patterns, variations in tones or rhythms, and sounds. They enjoy listening to music, composing music, interpreting music, performing to music, and learning with music playing in the background.

INTERPERSONAL DOMINANCE

Students with this dominant intelligence thrive on person-to-person interactions and team activities. They are sensitive to the feelings and needs of others and are skilled team members, discussion leaders, and peer mediators.

INTRAPERSONAL DOMINANCE

Students with this dominant intelligence prefer to work alone because they are self-reflective, self-motivated, and in tune with their own feelings, beliefs, strengths, and thought processes. They respond to intrinsic rather than extrinsic rewards and may demonstrate great wisdom and insight when presented with personal challenges and independent-study opportunities.

The Theory of Multiple Intelligences can be used as a guide for the teacher who is interested in creating lesson plans that address one or more of the intelligences on a daily basis. Teachers should ask themselves the following questions when attempting to develop or evaluate classroom activities using seven intelligences:

(1) What tasks require students to write, speak, or read?

(2) What tasks require students to engage in problem solving, logical thought, or calculations?

(3) What tasks require students to create images or visual aids and to analyze colors, textures, forms, or shapes?

(4) What tasks require students to employ body motions, manipulations, or hands-on approaches to learning?

(5) What tasks require students to incorporate music, rhythm, pitch, tones, or environmental sounds in their work?

(6) What tasks require students to work in groups and to interact with others?

(7) What tasks require students to express personal feelings, insights, beliefs, and self-disclosing ideas?

The following pages provide the teacher with several examples of how the Multiple Intelligences have been used as an organizing structure when designing classroom materials and assignments.

Learning Math by Using

Manipulatives

VERBAL/LINGUISTIC

Select one of the math manipulatives. Prepare a short demonstration speech to show how to use this learning tool to teach a math concept.

LOGICAL/MATHEMATICAL

Develop a sequential lesson plan that teaches a math concept using one or more of the math manipulatives.

VISUAL/SPATIAL

Complete a series of drawings or diagrams demonstrating the use of one or more of the math manipulatives to teach a math concept.

BODY/KINESTHETIC

Use one or more of the math manipulatives to teach a math concept to someone else in the class.

MUSICAL/RHYTHMIC

Use a series of drumbeats to accompany the use of one or more of the math manipulatives to teach a math concept. The drumbeats should reflect the use of the manipulatives in some way.

INTERPERSONAL

Work with a partner to prepare a simple exhibit or display showing how math manipulatives can be used to teach math concepts.

INTRAPERSONAL

Record ways that you might find math manipulatives to be helpful as you attempt to learn various math concepts.

MANIPULATIVES TO CONSIDER: tangrams, pattern blocks, cuisenaire rods, geoboards, fraction bars, protractors, compasses, measurement tools.

The Role of Mathematics in Working Lives

Mathematics at Work

VERBAL/LINGUISTIC

Prepare a brief essay describing how you use mathematics in your day-to-day activities at home and at school.

LOGICAL/MATHEMATICAL

Brainstorm a list of possible careers. Think of key mathematical concepts that would be important in the careers on your list; then list the concepts in order of importance for each career.

VISUAL/SPATIAL

Conduct a survey of workers in your school or community to determine different ways that math is important to many jobs.

BODY/KINESTHETIC

Create or design something that requires you to apply several different math concepts.

MUSICAL/RHYTHMIC

Discuss the many ways that math is important to a composer, to a conductor, and to a critic of musical productions.

INTERPERSONAL

Organize a panel discussion to share the many ways that mathematics is used in your art, music, physical education, home economics, industrial arts, and computer classes.

INTRAPERSONAL

Write a journal entry that tells how numbers are important in your life.

Mathematical Terms

The Language of Mathematics

VERBAL/LINGUISTIC
Compile a dictionary of important mathematical terms and their definitions. Put your dictionary in a booklet or file card format.

LOGICAL/MATHEMATICAL
Generate a list of important mathematical terms. Classify your list of words in at least three different ways.

VISUAL/SPATIAL
Create a picture glossary of as many different mathematical terms as you can by drawing examples of the terms rather than giving written definitions. Have others try to guess which concepts you are illustrating.

BODY/KINESTHETIC
Invent a game that teaches mathematical terms to other students. It can be a word game, board game, television game, or card game. Be sure to include rules for your game and guidelines for playing the game.

MUSICAL/RHYTHMIC
Develop a mini-poster of musical terms that can also be used as mathematical terms.

INTERPERSONAL
Work with a partner to prepare a series of journal entries that might have been written by a mathematician who is working to make the language or terms of mathematics appealing to students.

INTRAPERSONAL
Illustrate at least three of your favorite math words in creative or personalized ways.

Using a Calculator

The Classic Calculator

VERBAL/LINGUISTIC

Pretend you work for a company that manufactures calculators. Your job is to write a "how to" card that tells how to operate a calculator. Write step-by-step directions for buyers of the calculator.

LOGICAL/MATHEMATICAL

As an employee of a calculator manufacturing company, you have been hired to solve problems that may arise when using a calculator. Outline a detailed plan for educating consumers on solving these problems. What marketing strategies will you use and what calculator "tricks and shortcuts" will you emphasize?

VISUAL/SPATIAL

Your role in your calculator manufacturing company is to create meaningful diagrams that show the different parts of a calculator, complete with labels and simple directions for use.

BODY/KINESTHETIC

Role play the part of a salesperson of a local company that manufactures calculators. The salesperson is showing a group of prospective buyers how the product works.

MUSICAL/RHYTHMIC

Pretend you are preparing a radio advertisement for a company that manufactures calculators. Write a short "blurb" describing the uses of a calculator, and then experiment with different kinds of introductory and/or background music in a search to find the best music for eliciting a positive response to the ad.

INTERPERSONAL

Work with a partner to make a case for the widespread use of calculators in the classroom. This argument should be one that could be used by a calculator manufacturing company to promote the sale of its product in school districts across the country.

INTRAPERSONAL

Write a personal letter to a mock company that manufactures calculators telling the employees how you feel about the use of calculators in the teaching and learning of math concepts.

Use of Numbers

Newspaper Numbers

VERBAL/LINGUISTIC
Scan the local newspaper to see how different types of numbers are used in various sections. Write your findings in a short report, including examples.

LOGICAL/MATHEMATICAL
Scan the local newspaper to see how different types of numbers are used in various sections. Tally your results for each section and show your findings in chart or graph form.

VISUAL/SPATIAL
Scan the local newspaper to see how different types of numbers are used in various sections. Clip out a variety of ads, articles, diagrams, charts, graphs, and other items that make use of numbers to document your findings. Paste these in a mini-scrapbook, adding appropriate labels and brief explanations.

BODY/KINESTHETIC
Scan the local newspaper to see how different types of numbers are used in various sections. Prepare a transparency talk to share your findings with others in the class.

MUSICAL/RHYTHMIC
Scan the local newspaper to see how different types of numbers are used in various sections. Create a sound/tonal-based legend or index for each number category found in your newspaper survey.

INTERPERSONAL
Scan the local newspaper to see how different types of numbers are used in various sections. Work with a partner to create riddles about specific number applications you have discovered. Others should be able to use the riddles to locate the number types.

INTRAPERSONAL
Scan the local newspaper to see how different types of numbers are used in various sections. Write a "number autobiography," using several types of numbers to describe yourself.

Famous Mathematicians

Mathematicians Are Real People

 VERBAL/LINGUISTIC
Research these mathematicians and write a short paragraph describing the major mathematical contribution of each: Lagrange, Descartes, Newton, Archimedes, Euclid, Pythagoras, and Fibonacci.

 LOGICAL/MATHEMATICAL
Research these mathematicians and construct a short timeline recording five major events in each life: Lagrange, Descartes, Newton, Archimedes, Euclid, Pythagoras, and Fibonacci.

 VISUAL/SPATIAL
Research these mathematicians and paint a mural showing important events related to math in the life of each: Lagrange, Descartes, Newton, Archimedes, Euclid, Pythagoras, and Fibonacci.

 BODY/KINESTHETIC
Research these mathematicians and act out a series of short scenarios depicting a significant activity in the life of each one: Lagrange, Descartes, Newton, Archimedes, Euclid, Pythagoras, and Fibonacci.

 **MUSICAL/RHYTHMIC**
Work with a partner who is completing an activity from one of the other intelligences. Select music pieces to play in the background as he or she conducts the research.

 **INTERPERSONAL**
Research these mathematicians and then stage a series of mock interviews with each individual to discover his or her contribution to the world of mathematics: Lagrange, Descartes, Newton, Archimedes, Euclid, Pythagoras, and Fibonacci.

 **INTRAPERSONAL**
Research these mathematicians and imagine the advice each would give a math student today : Lagrange, Descartes, Newton, Archimedes, Euclid, Pythagoras, and Fibonacci.

Types of Numbers

Name That Number

VERBAL/LINGUISTIC

Stage a "mathematical spelling bee" for small groups of students in your class. The students should be required to spell each of the following types of numbers, and to give an example of each: **whole, cardinal, ordinal, prime, even, odd, composite, positive, negative, fractional, rational,** and **irrational.**

LOGICAL/MATHEMATICAL

Create a series of number patterns. Have a friend finish the sequences. Try to reflect as many of the number types as you can that are mentioned in the Verbal/Linguistic activity.

VISUAL/SPATIAL

Draw a picture of a specific setting or scenario using various number types as the focus or theme of the picture. Try to reflect the number types mentioned in the Verbal/Linguistic activity.

BODY/KINESTHETIC

Make a set of flash cards showing the correct spelling and definition of each type of number listed in the Verbal/Linguistic activity. Include an example of each number on the appropriate card.

MUSICAL/RHYTHMIC

Make up a set of sounds, beats, or rhythmic patterns that represent the different types of numbers listed in the Verbal/Linguistic activity.

INTERPERSONAL

Work with a partner to develop a quiz that would test one's understanding of the different types of numbers listed in the Verbal/Linguistic activity.

INTRAPERSONAL

Write a brief statement answering each of the following questions:

1. Are you more like a whole number or a fractional number?
2. Are you more like a prime number or a composite number?
3. Are you more like a positive number or a negative number?
4. Are you more like a rational number or an irrational number?

18

Mathematical Operations

Operation Math

Choose one of the following mathematical operations to use as the basis for completing each of the following activities:

1. Calculating ratios or percentages
2. Adding or subtracting fractions
3. Multiplying or dividing fractions
4. Adding or subtracting decimals
5. Multiplying or dividing decimals

VERBAL/LINGUISTIC
Write a detailed paragraph explaining how to perform the mathematical operation you have selected.

LOGICAL/MATHEMATICAL
Outline the steps for completing the mathematical operation.

VISUAL/SPATIAL
Draw a diagram showing the process for performing the mathematical operation.

BODY/KINESTHETIC
Use manipulatives to demonstrate the mathematical operation.

MUSICAL/RHYTHMIC
Make up a jingle, rap, or song to help someone learn the mathematical operation.

INTERPERSONAL
Work with a partner. "Each one teach one" the mathematical operation.

INTRAPERSONAL
Tell whether or not the operation you selected was difficult for you. Explain why or why not.

Sets

Are You Set in Your Ways? Page 1

In order to complete the following activities, first select a topic from a science or social studies unit that you are studying at the present time. For example, in science you might choose the topic of the solar system, or that of rocks and minerals. A social studies topic choice might be battles of the Civil War period, or colonies and territories of nations at particular times in history.

Remember that a set is a collection of items, and that there are three types of sets: equal sets, equivalent sets, and subsets. Also remember that we can use sets to look at topics in different ways. This occurs when we look at an intersection of sets, or when we describe a union of sets.

VERBAL/LINGUISTIC

In a short written paper, use sets to describe the elements of your science or social studies topic. Include the following in your descriptions:

1. Members of a set
2. Equal sets
3. Equivalent sets
4. Subsets
5. Intersection of sets (using a Venn diagram)
6. Null or empty set

LOGICAL/MATHEMATICAL

Determine how set theory can help you compare and contrast different members of a set. Explain your ideas as they pertain to your science or social studies topic.

VISUAL/SPATIAL

Construct a series of diagrams to illustrate each of the following as they can be used to help explain your science or social studies topic:

1. Members of a set
2. Equal sets
3. Equivalent sets
4. Subsets
5. Intersection of sets (using a Venn diagram)
6. Null or empty set

Are You Set in Your Ways? Page 2

BODY/KINESTHETIC
Draw a set of pictures to represent each of the following as they pertain to your science or social studies topic:

1. Members of a set
2. Equal sets
3. Equivalent sets
4. Subsets
5. Intersection of sets (using a Venn diagram)
6. Null or empty set

MUSICAL/RHYTHMIC
Make up a creative or interpretive dance to demonstrate the different dimensions of set theory.

INTERPERSONAL
Perform the following role play: a mathematics teacher showing his or her class how to apply set theory to a science or social studies topic.

INTRAPERSONAL
Write a journal entry answering these questions: "What are my feelings about using set theory to study science or social studies? Is it a helpful educational strategy or not?"

Numbers in Sports

Sporting Mathematics

VERBAL/LINGUISTIC

Write a creative story using the theme of numbers in sports. Choose one of the following titles:

- **The High Scoring Game**
- **Numbers Don't Tell It All**
- **Going the Extra Mile**
- **Time Is Money**
- **The Day I Outdistanced My Opponent**

LOGICAL/MATHEMATICAL

Construct a chart showing how numbers are used in four to six different sports such as baseball, football, soccer, hockey, basketball, or tennis. Consider everything from scores and rules to times and distances.

VISUAL/SPATIAL

Draw diagrams to scale of at least six different playing fields for sports of your choice. Label these diagrams with the correct measurements. Be sure to provide a key for your scale drawings.

BODY/KINESTHETIC

Stage a sporting contest for a game of your choice. Prepare a poster advertising and promoting the event, including as many different numbers in the message as you can.

MUSICAL/RHYTHMIC

Record a musical collage of popular songs associated with various sporting events.

INTERPERSONAL

Work with a partner to poll members of your class to determine their favorite sports to watch or to play. Graph your results.

INTRAPERSONAL

Pretend you have set a world record for kids in a sport of your choice. Compose a letter to your best friend, telling him or her how you did it, using numbers to make your key points.

Math Anxiety and Test Scores

Dealing with Math Anxiety

VERBAL/LINGUISTIC

Write a short essay describing how you think students generally feel about math classes and math tests. You may conduct some informal interviews with students before writing this essay.

LOGICAL/MATHEMATICAL

Develop a student math handbook that gives students helpful hints on the following topics: (1) important math terms to know; (2) steps to take when studying for a math test; (3) ways to reduce test anxiety; (4) sample math problems for you to know how to solve; and (5) math tricks and tidbits.

VISUAL/SPATIAL

Prepare a "math cue chart" of important math ideas and facts for you to keep in your math textbook or math notebook at all times. This "legal cheat sheet" should be a good reference for you to use when completing math assignments.

BODY/KINESTHETIC

Role play two scenarios where students are getting ready to take a math test. Use one scenario to show how students are preparing for the test in positive ways. The other scenario should show students who are not preparing properly for the test.

MUSICAL/RHYTHMIC

Select appropriate music that could be played in the background during a math study session or a math testing situation. Determine if this music relaxes students or distracts students during these sessions.

INTERPERSONAL

Stage a panel discussion, using a panel of good math students who can share their personal experiences, study hints, study habits, and methods for solving problems with the class.

INTRAPERSONAL

Relate a positive or a negative experience that you have had in a math class. Tell how you felt and why you felt as you did.

Using Learning Stations as an Instructional Tool

Learning stations come in every size, shape, and color, and can be placed in ordinary or unusual locations. A learning station can be as simple as a bulletin board station that is used by students for extra credit when their regular work is done, or as sophisticated as a series of technology stations around which the entire classroom program is organized. Learning stations can be used for teaching content or practicing skills on a daily basis, weekly basis, monthly basis, or for an entire semester.

The principal importance of a learning station is that it is a physical area where students engage in a variety of learning activities. An effective learning station (1) includes multilevel tasks; (2) offers choices in and alternatives to the tasks it requires; (3) is attractive and motivational; (4) provides clear directions and procedures; (5) accommodates three to five students at one sitting; (6) has flexible time limitations for completion; (7) controls and coordinates movement to and from or between stations; (8) incorporates varied learning styles, modalities, and intelligences; (9) manages student participation through record-keeping strategies; and (10) encourages authentic types of assessment through the use of products and portfolios.

Some of the best formats for learning stations are:

- File folders
- Bulletin boards
- Pocket packets
- Portable desktop centers
- Shoeboxes
- Recipe boxes

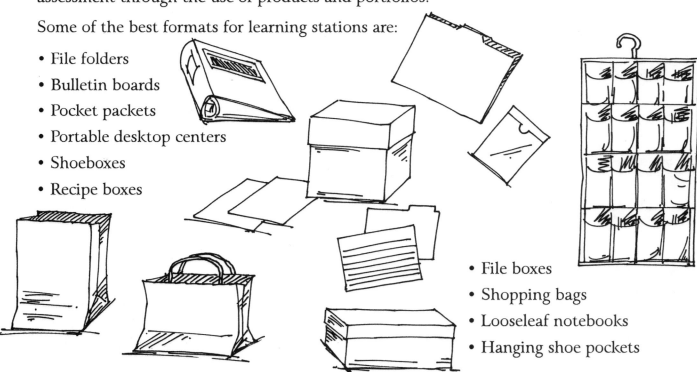

- File boxes
- Shopping bags
- Looseleaf notebooks
- Hanging shoe pockets

For more examples and explanations of learning station formats, see *Interdisciplinary Units and Projects for Thematic Instruction* by Imogene Forte and Sandra Schurr, Incentive Publications, 1995.

Some of the most practical ways to use space when setting up learning stations are the following:

Arrange desks in clusters of four or six.

Place an easel between two desks (or place two desks on each side of the easel).

Use bulletin boards or hanging displays in strategic positions.

Use round tables.

Place bookcases at an angle in a corner of the room, adjacent to clustered desks or round tables.

25

Use backs of bookcases, teacher's desk, or other large pieces of furniture.

Arrange lap boards made of masonite or plywood around a carpeted area where students can sit on the floor.

Some evaluative techniques for use with learning stations that could become products and artifacts for a portfolio are:

- Anecdotal records
- Games, quizzes, puzzles
- Logs and diaries
- Teacher- or student-made tests
- Class or individual charts, graphs
- Checklists
- Tape recordings
- Suggestion boxes
- Scrapbooks or notebooks
- Observation records
- Interviews
- Conferences
- Student rating scales
- Daily progress reports
- Library pockets with individual reporting cards

Finally, here are some things that should be considered before setting up learning stations in the middle level classroom:

1 Decide what you want to teach at each station. Write one or more student objectives. These should be things the student should do in order to show that he or she understands the concept or skill presented.

2 Decide on optional strategies, activities, and tasks for teaching those objectives.

3 Locate all supporting tools and materials for completing the assigned and/or optional tasks. Be sure that students know which materials are included in the station, how to use the materials, and how to care for them.

4 Write specific directions, procedures, and explanations for doing the work at the station. Give students an estimated timetable for completion of the station.

5 Plan for "traffic flow" in relation to other activities that will take place while the station is in use. Plan also for scheduling students into use of the stations. There are many ways to do this. Students can be scheduled to attend each station on a specific rotation. Provided there is room at a new station, students can move on to that station when they are finished with an assigned station. If the stations or station tasks are flexible and portable, students can take them to their seats. Finally, students can sign up for stations based on their interests and/or learning needs.

6 Introduce all station themes or names and the character and major content of each station before students actually begin tackling station activities. Be specific when you tell students what your expectations are in terms of their performance or achievement at each station, and be sure students understand how their achievements will be assessed. As part of this process, provide checkpoints where students may go for help should they forget or misunderstand initial instructions, or where students may review the information presented in this introduction.

Using the Read and Relate Concept as an Instructional Tool

Read and Relate activities require the student to read or review a set of important concepts in a given subject area and then to use these concepts as springboards for applying a range of creative or critical thinking skills.

Using the textbook or a favorite set of alternative reference materials, the teacher begins the Read and Relate process by selecting a number of ideas related to a topic that is being taught as part of an instructional unit. These ideas should be representative of key facts that will be learned by the student. It is crucial that these ideas lend themselves easily to a number of extended reading, writing, or thinking exercises that can provide opportunities for students to apply the facts in a new and different context.

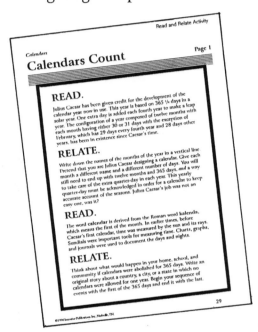

Once the teacher has generated a list, the concepts are written as a series of short, descriptive paragraphs to be reviewed by the student. The paragraphs should be approximately three to five sentences in length, and they should be presented in a logical or sequential manner.

Next, teachers should use Bloom's Taxonomy, Williams' Taxonomy, or any of Gardner's Multiple Intelligences as a basis for developing a follow-up reading, writing, speaking, or thinking activity for each factual paragraph. The activity should require the student to "do something" with the concept in a new and different way. The intent of this instructional strategy is to help the student understand that many important ideas learned in one subject area can be related to ideas in another subject area.

Notice how each descriptive paragraph is followed by a special application challenge for students to complete.

Calendars

Calendars Count

READ.

Julius Caesar has been given credit for the development of the calendar year now in use. This year is based on 365 ¼ days in a solar year. One extra day is added each fourth year to make a leap year. The configuration of a year composed of twelve months with each month having either 30 or 31 days with the exception of February, which has 29 days every fourth year and 28 days other years, has been in existence since Caesar's time.

RELATE.

Write down the names of the months of the year in a vertical line. Pretend that you are Julius Caesar designing a calendar. Give each month a different name and a different number of days. You will still need to end up with twelve months and 365 days, *and* a way to take care of the extra quarter-day in each year. This yearly quarter-day must be acknowledged in order for a calendar to keep accurate account of the seasons. Julius Caesar's job was not an easy one, was it?

READ.

The word **calendar** is derived from the Roman word **kalenda**, which means the first of the month. In earlier times, before Caesar's first calendar, time was measured by the sun and its rays. Sundials were important tools for measuring time. Charts, graphs, and journals were used to document the days and nights.

RELATE.

Think about what would happen in your home, school, and community if calendars were abolished for 365 days. Write an original story about a country, a city, or a state in which no calendars were allowed for one year. Begin your sequence of events with the first of the 365 days and end it with the last.

Calendars Count

READ.

January is considered by many people to be the most important month of the year because it is the first month. Being first has become an important part of world culture. January 1, New Year's Day, has become a symbol of "starting over" and a time for making resolutions related to improving the quality of one's life during the forthcoming year.

RELATE.

Take a new look at your calendar and devise a creative way to give positive importance to a different month of the year. Think of a way to focus attention on the second, third, seventh, or any month of the year. Maybe you'd like to take the month in which you were born or the month school or vacation begins. Establish a "cause" for your month (examples: nature, learning, relationships), a special holiday, and other distinguishing features.

READ.

The ancient Babylonians studied the stars and kept accurate records over long periods of time of their discoveries. Their records were then used to create early calendars. Users of today's calendars owe a debt of appreciation to these early scientists. It was their dedication and hard work that led to the development of the calendar that we take for granted as an indispensable tool for daily living.

RELATE.

Design a calendar with an astrological theme in honor of the early Babylonians. Use reference materials to find information on the stars to use in creating your illustrations. Be creative, but also be accurate in your portrayal of the wonders of the nighttime sky.

Using Integrated Instructional Strategies to Develop Problem-solving and Higher-order Thinking Skills

Using Bloom's Taxonomy as an Instructional Tool

Bloom's Taxonomy is a well-known model for teaching critical thinking skills in any subject area. Based on the work of Benjamin Bloom, the taxonomy consists of six different thinking levels arranged in a hierarchy of difficulty.

Any student can function at each level of the taxonomy provided the content is appropriate for his or her reading ability. In order for teachers to consistently design lesson plans that incorporate all six levels, they should use the taxonomy to structure all student objectives, all information sessions, all questions, all assigned tasks, and all items on tests.

On the opposite page is a brief summary of the six taxonomy levels with a list of common student behaviors, presented as action verbs, associated with each level. When developing learning tasks and activities around Bloom's Taxonomy, it is important to include in each set at least one activity for each level of the taxonomy. Keep a copy of the Bloom's page in your lesson planning book so it will be handy when you need it.

Bloom's Taxonomy can be used to structure sets of learning tasks, student worksheets, cooperative learning group assignments, and independent study units. On the following pages you will find a collection of learning assignments based on this taxonomy. Topics were selected to be appealing to students and to blend into a middle grades curriculum.

Bloom's Taxonomy of Critical Thought

KNOWLEDGE LEVEL: Learn the information.

Sample Verbs: Define, find, follow directions, identify, know, label, list, memorize, name, quote, read, recall, recite, recognize, select, state, write.

COMPREHENSION LEVEL: Understand the information.

Sample Verbs: Account for, explain, express in other terms, give examples, give in own words, group, illustrate, infer, interpret, paraphrase, recognize, retell, show, simplify, summarize, translate.

APPLICATION LEVEL: Use the information.

Sample Verbs: Apply, compute, construct, construct using, convert (in math), demonstrate, derive, develop, discuss, generalize, interview, investigate, keep records, model, participate, perform, plan, produce, prove (in math), solve, use, utilize.

ANALYSIS LEVEL: Break the information down into its component parts.

Sample Verbs: Analyze, compare, contrast, criticize, debate, determine, diagram, differentiate, discover, draw conclusions, examine, infer, relate, search, sort, survey, take apart, uncover.

SYNTHESIS LEVEL: Put information together in new and different ways.

Sample Verbs: Build, combine, create, design, imagine, invent, make up, present, produce, propose.

EVALUATION LEVEL: Judge the information.

Sample Verbs: Assess, defend, evaluate, grade, judge, measure, perform a critique, rank, recommend, select, test, validate, verify.

Everyday Use of Mathematics

Math in Daily Life

KNOWLEDGE

Make a list of all the ways you can think of that you use math in your daily life.

COMPREHENSION

Explain some special ways math is used by people in the following professions:
- teacher • doctor • letter carrier

Now think of ways math is used by three other people you come into contact with on a regular basis.

SYNTHESIS

Create a set of question-and-answer cards about occupations and hobbies that are dependent on math skills and knowledge. Use the cards to design a trivia or board game. Question cards might include: **What special math tools are required by a designer of bridges? Name three occupations that are highly dependent on an advanced knowledge of computers. What special mathematical skills does a scuba diver need?**

APPLICATION

Make a list of tools with mathematical foundations that are in use in your home or school. Many of these tools, such as clocks, calendars, and scales, are so taken for granted that they are often unnoticed as a regular part of our environment.

ANALYSIS

Do you think that in the next few years scientists will devise computers or other high-tech products whose use will completely replace the math systems you are learning now? Write an essay for class discussion stating your opinion and giving reasons for it.

EVALUATION

Interview ten people of your parents' generation to compare their middle school math education with your own. Think about how modern technology influenced their need for math skills in the world of work, and then estimate the math needs of your generation as you enter the work force.

$5+3$

Catalogs

Mail-order Math

KNOWLEDGE

Review a collection of mail-order catalogs to find out how many different ways math skills and processes have been used in the presentation of each catalog (examples: pricing, space allocation, number of products on a page, postage). List all the ways you can.

COMPREHENSION

Select three pages in one catalog that contain similar products. Add the cost of the items on each page and compare all three totals. Then add the three totals together and divide the sum by the total number of items on the three pages in order to determine the average cost per item for those three pages.

APPLICATION

Prepare an eight- to ten-page catalog featuring consumer products which would be of interest to people of your age. Write catalog descriptions and give prices, including shipping costs, for all items. For each item, calculate the percentage of total cost constituted by the shipping charges.

SYNTHESIS

Develop plans for a new type of catalog aimed at the family market. It should be based on applications of the computer, television, telemarketing, or another form of modern technology.

ANALYSIS

Use advertisements from a local newspaper to locate products similar to those in one or more of your catalogs. Compare the prices of products sold in your local stores to prices of products in the catalogs. Taking into account shipping and handling charges for the catalog and transportation costs for local shopping, determine which is the most economical way to buy the selected products.

EVALUATION

Prepare a checklist that class members can use when evaluating catalogs, selecting products based on quality and competitive pricing, and completing order forms.

Statistics

Mean, Median, and Mode

KNOWLEDGE
Define **mean, median,** and **mode.**

COMPREHENSION
Give examples of how the terms **mean, median,** and **mode** are used in math.

APPLICATION
Make a list of things that you like to do at home, at school, or in the community. Label each item on your list with a **1, 2, 3,** or **4,** using this rating scale: **4 = would like to do it all of the time; 3 = would like to do it most of the time; 2 = would like to do it some of the time; 1 = would like to do it a very few times.** Find the mean of the ratings of the items on your list. Find the median by placing the numbers in order from largest rating to smallest rating. What is the mode? Remember that the mode is the number that occurs most often. Sometimes there is no mode, and sometimes there is more than one mode.

SYNTHESIS
Imagine a perfect school day during which you could do whatever you wanted from morning until two hours after the end of the school day. Create a circle graph for an eight-hour day showing how you would spend your time. Provide specific time frames for each activity.

EVALUATION
Discuss your understanding of the terms **mean, median,** and **mode** with a classmate. Include in the discussion your interpretation of these terms as they influence your daily life and school work. Compare your perceptions with those of your friend.

ANALYSIS
Compare and contrast the items from your Application list that are rated **4** with those that are rated **1.** What seems to account for most of the differences?

Graphs

Getting a Grip on Graphs

KNOWLEDGE
Make a list of as many kinds of graphs as you can.

APPLICATION
Construct a list of questions about a topic on which you have a strong opinion. Assuming an impartial attitude, use your list of questions to conduct a survey of your classmates in order to discover *their* opinions. Show the results of your survey with a colorful graph of your own design.

COMPREHENSION
Give brief descriptions of at least five different kinds of graphs.

SYNTHESIS
Decide which would be the best way to organize findings about consumer spending for a social studies report: a circle graph, a bar graph, or a broken-line graph. Justify your decision.

ANALYSIS
Distinguish between a bar graph and a double bar graph. Give an example of a good use of each.

EVALUATION
Defend or criticize this statement as it applies to the use of a pictograph to show comparisons: "One picture is worth a thousand words."

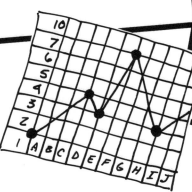

Studying Geometry

Geometry on the Line

KNOWLEDGE

Make an alphabetical listing of these terms that are frequently used in geometry: **point, line, line segment, parallel lines, skew lines, intersecting lines, congruent line segments, plane, ray.**

APPLICATION

Name the geometric figure that is suggested by each of the following:
- a flashlight's beam
- the edge of your math book
- a windowpane
- a baseball bat

COMPREHENSION

Use resource materials to find definitions for words important in the study of geometry. Use your own words to write a definition beside each word. In this way you can begin building a geometry study guide for your notebook.

SYNTHESIS

Review your textbooks and available resource materials to prepare an annotated bibliography of study helps, examples, practice exercises, and problem-solving strategies and procedures to help you in your pursuit of geometry mastery.

ANALYSIS

Cut or tear paper models to demonstrate each of the terms defined in your geometry study guide. Try to determine similarities and differences in the various models.

EVALUATION

Make up a list of questions or concerns you have about your own understanding of geometry and its application to your daily life. Discuss your list with your teacher and develop a plan of action for further study.

38

Fractions

Freaky Fractions

KNOWLEDGE

Using your own words, write a definition of **fraction**.

APPLICATION

Give examples of three times you have used fractions in your daily life within the last week.

COMPREHENSION

Write the following fractions as numerals, each accompanied by a sketch or illustration:

- two and five-twelfths
- sixteen and one-third
- one piece of pie from a pie that is divided into eight parts
- five whole apples plus two parts of another apple that is divided into thirds

ANALYSIS

Determine what makes fractions easier or harder for students to learn when compared with other math topics such as geometry, decimals, and whole numbers.

SYNTHESIS

Compile a study guide for your notebook to help with your continued study of fractions. Include tips, shortcuts, procedures, and references.

EVALUATION

Survey twenty classmates to determine which of the following is the most popular spectator sport: football, basketball, baseball, hockey, tennis, golf, or swimming. Make a bar graph to show the results of your study. Give the fraction of the twenty people that chose each sport.

Estimating

Estimation Expert

KNOWLEDGE

Use your dictionary to locate the precise definition of the word **estimate**. Write down the definition. Then write definitions of **estimated**, **estimator**, and **estimation**. Does each word mean exactly what you thought it did?

COMPREHENSION

Explain the importance of **rounding off, random sampling, comparison,** and **clustering** in the estimating process.

ANALYSIS

Compare and contrast **estimation, guesstimation,** and **prediction.**

APPLICATION

Estimate:
- tomorrow's temperature for your city
- the average daily attendance for your class for this week
- the time the sun will set in your back-yard tonight
- your grade for your next math quiz

EVALUATION

Tell how each of the following people would need to use estimation in daily life. Then rank the people in the list to show the importance of estimation skills to success in each field:

- a rocket scientist
- a dressmaker
- a television producer
- an investigative journalist
- a middle school principal
- a chef
- an airline pilot

SYNTHESIS

Write a fictitious account of a situation in which estimation was used unwisely and without proper consideration. Build a sequence of events to show the point at which the decision based on estimation was made. From there, move to a climax revealing the results of the decision.

Time Zones

Time Out

KNOWLEDGE

Define the following: **prime meridian, Greenwich Mean Time,** and **Universal Time.**

COMPREHENSION

Explain how travelers should adjust their watches when traveling west across time zones. How should they adjust their watches when traveling east across time zones?

SYNTHESIS

Use one of the following ideas to develop a plot for a TV situation comedy:

- Traveling in a westward direction around the world, a traveler crosses the International Date Line twice in one week—and forgets to change his or her watch both times.

- A teenager telephones someone he or she met on a summer vacation, calling three or four times a day, forgetting about the six-hour time difference between their cities.

- A research scientist is assigned to find a better way to establish world time zones employing modern technology.

APPLICATION

Look at a world map that shows all the time zones. Use the map to find out how far it is from your own time zone to the time zone that is farthest from you. What is the difference (in hours) between these two time zones?

EVALUATION

Evaluate the importance of standard time zones in the areas of world traffic, commerce, and people's everyday lives. Mention some of the problems that would occur were there no standard time zones.

ANALYSIS

Make a study of the boundaries of the world's time zones. Try to find out why particular boundaries were established. (For example, why are many time zone boundaries irregular?)

Measurement Systems

Measuring Up

KNOWLEDGE

Create your own measurement dictionary by defining the following words: **unit, inch, foot, yard, mile, millimeter, centimeter, meter, kilometer, cup, pint, quart, gallon, liter, second, minute, hour, day, week, month, year, decade, century, ounce, pound, ton, milligram, gram,** and **kilogram.**

APPLICATION

Select a recipe you would like to prepare for your family. Use resource materials to help you translate the standard U.S. measurements to metric measurements. Copy the entire recipe using the metric measurements. Remember, if you want to prepare the recipe using metric measurements, you will need to have access to a metric scale and a calibrated liter container.

COMPREHENSION

Categorize each of the words in your measurement dictionary in at least two different ways.

OR

Give examples of how you have used ten measurement devices defined in your dictionary within the past month. Try to think of another way you could have completed each task had the measurement tool not been available.

Measuring Up

ANALYSIS

If you had to complete your schoolwork, home chores, and recreational projects for the next year with the use of only ten measurement tools from your list, which ten would you choose? Write a short paragraph explaining your choices and reflecting on how your normal daily routine might be affected.

EVALUATION

Design a skit for the class to demonstrate the use of a set of measuring tools in a very unusual and entertaining setting.

Examples:

- weighing and measuring an elephant

- baking cakes for the entire student body of your school

- determining the weight and length of a grasshopper

- determining how much fabric to buy to make costumes for four classmates who will dress as your school mascot for an open house at your school—one classmate is six feet, one inch tall and weighs 160 pounds; one is four feet, two inches tall and weighs ninety pounds; the other two are five feet, five inches tall and weigh about 125 pounds each

SYNTHESIS

Reflect on how accurate measurements can lead to different results from measurements made by estimation. Draw a cartoon or comic strip to show a situation in which estimation or "guesstimation" led to some unexpected results.

Using Williams' Taxonomy as an Instructional Tool

Williams' Taxonomy is another important model to use when teaching thinking skills. While Bloom's Taxonomy is used for teaching critical thinking skills, Williams' Taxonomy is used for teaching creative thinking skills.

Although there is a relationship between these two models, and even some overlap, it should be noted that critical thinking tends to be more reactive and vertical in nature while creative thinking tends to be more proactive and lateral in nature. Another way of saying this is that critical thinking tends to involve tasks that are logical, rational, sequential, analytical, and convergent. Creative thinking, on the other hand, tends to involve tasks that are spatial, flexible, spontaneous, analogical, and divergent. Critical thinking is "left brain" thinking while creative thinking is "right brain" thinking.

Williams' Taxonomy has eight levels, also arranged in a hierarchy, with certain types of student behavior associated with each level. The first four levels of the Williams' model are cognitive in nature while the last four levels are affective in nature.

It is strongly suggested that a teacher keep a copy of Williams' Taxonomy in the lesson plan book so that the levels and behaviors can be an integral part of most lesson plans and student assignments. On the opposite page is a brief overview of the levels in Williams' Taxonomy. Each level is accompanied by a few cue words to be used to trigger student responses to a given creative stimulus or challenge.

The following pages offer a wide variety of student worksheets, assignments, independent study guides, or group problem-solving tasks, covering many different content areas appropriate for middle grade classrooms.

Williams' Taxonomy of Creative Thought

FLUENCY

Enables the learner to generate a great many ideas, related answers, or choices in a given situation.

Sample Cue Words: Generating oodles, lots, many ideas.

FLEXIBILITY

Lets the learner change everyday objects to generate a variety of categories by taking detours and varying sizes, shapes, quantities, time limits, requirements, objectives, or dimensions in a given situation.

Sample Cue Words: Generating varied, different, alternative ideas.

ORIGINALITY

Causes the learner to seek new ideas by suggesting unusual twists to change content or by coming up with clever responses to a given situation.

Sample Cue Words: Generating unusual, unique, new ideas.

ELABORATION

Helps the learner stretch by expanding, enlarging, enriching, or embellishing possibilities that build on previous thoughts or ideas.

Sample Cue Words: Generating enriched, embellished, expanded ideas.

RISK TAKING

Enables the learner to deal with the unknown by taking chances, experimenting with new ideas, or trying new challenges.

Sample Cue Words: Experimenting with and exploring ideas.

COMPLEXITY

Permits the learner to create structure in an unstructured setting or to build a logical order in a given situation.

Sample Cue Words: Improving and explaining ideas.

CURIOSITY

Encourages the learner to follow a hunch, question alternatives, ponder outcomes, and wonder about options in a given situation.

Sample Cue Words: Pondering and questioning ideas.

IMAGINATION

Allows the learner to visualize possibilities, build images in his or her mind, picture new objects, or reach beyond the limits of the practical.

Sample Cue Words: Visualizing and fantasizing ideas.

Calculators

Calculator Countdown

Page 1

 FLUENCY
Brainstorm a list of jobs that can be made easier through the use of a calculator. As you make your list of jobs, write a brief job description for each.

 FLEXIBILITY
Think of and list ways that students of your age can expand their mastery of the calculator in order to be more successful students while acquiring skills necessary for the world of work.

 ORIGINALITY
Review available calculator games and activities and create a brand-new game to teach beginning use of the calculator to younger and less mature students.

 ELABORATION
Describe how you think math classes in your school would be affected if there were no calculators in use in the entire school. How do you think those who work in the administrative offices of your school would be affected if *they* were unable to use calculators for anything?

 RISK TAKING
Write a brief essay to convince your school's teachers and administrators to allow the use of calculators during achievement, aptitude, and intelligence tests.

 COMPLEXITY
Describe how the functions of computers and calculators differ. How do the two complement each other as parts of a complete math program?

Calculator Countdown

Page 2

 CURIOSITY

In which of the following situations do you think calculators are more important to students of your age?

- operations with fractions

- operations with place values

- general arithmetic

- puzzles and games

 IMAGINATION

Design and show a rough sketch of the keyboard and user's manual of a "super-duper calculator of the future." This calculator would serve to enrich and enhance middle grade math programs for every student, from the "math whizzes" to the "I hate math" students in your class. In which category do you fall?

Probability

A High Probability

 FLUENCY
Solve a probability problem by quickly listing all the permutations that you can. (Sample problem: How many permutations of a set of fruit consisting of an apple, an orange, and a banana are possible? Remember that a permutation is an *ordered* arrangement of a set of objects.)

 FLEXIBILITY
Now use a different approach. Use reason, or logic, to solve the permutation problem described in the Fluency activity.

 ORIGINALITY
Write a paragraph describing how you think the idea of probability may have occurred to a mathematician. (Then do some research to see how Pascal and Fermat developed their theory of probability.)

 ELABORATION
Elaborate on this starter statement: **"A good reason to study the nature of random events is . . ."**

 RISK TAKING
Tell if the theory of probability makes sense to you.

 COMPLEXITY
Tell why it is legal for an insurance company to set individual insurance rates based on probability rules even though an event predicted for a particular individual may never actually occur.

 CURIOSITY
What would you like to know about real-life applications of probability theory?

 IMAGINATION
Write a short story about a person who triumphs in a competitive situation by using his or her knowledge of the laws of probability.

Tessellations

Mathematical Artistry

 FLUENCY
Design a poster that defines and illustrates the concept of tessellations.

 FLEXIBILITY
A Dutch artist named M.C. Escher combined art and mathematics to create tessellations that have become well-known and respected by people all over the world. Research the life and works of M.C. Escher and construct a timeline to show how his life's work developed.

 ORIGINALITY
Many of M.C. Escher's tessellations have been used to develop commercial products. These products are often sold in museum or specialty shops, and include clothing as well as decorative objects. Illustrate some new and creative ways to use tessellations.

 ELABORATION
Design a brochure based on tessellations to advertise a series of consumer products for people of your age.

 RISK TAKING
Design a tessellation of your own. Cut your tessellations into puzzle pieces to be put together by a friend. Make your puzzle as attractive and challenging as possible.

 COMPLEXITY
Tessellations are actually mosaics. Describe how mosaics and collages are alike and different. Write a brief paragraph describing these differences and similarities.

 CURIOSITY
How do the study and use of tessellations help a student understand geometry?

 IMAGINATION
Sketch the outline of a tessellation that would be appropriate for a birthday or holiday card or a card of congratulations for a special friend. Write an original poem to accompany your greeting card.

Mathematics and Computers

Math and the Computer

 FLUENCY
Make a list of all the ways a computer could help you in your math classes.

 FLEXIBILITY
Are there some things a computer can do that might help you solve math problems more quickly but might at the same time keep you from acquiring in-depth knowledge of some areas of math? Classify the items on your list according to a system that acknowledges this possibility.

 ORIGINALITY
Using the graphics program on your classroom computer, create an original design, relying on math concepts such as measurement and geometric shapes. Discuss the mathematical elements of your design.

 ELABORATION
Create a dictionary of ten math terms that have particular relevance to the world of computers. Design a crossword puzzle using the terms.

 RISK TAKING
Do you like (or would you like) to perform mathematical tasks with the help of a computer? Tell how you feel about using technology in this way.

 COMPLEXITY
Examine the topic of artificial intelligence. A sophisticated computer program may answer your questions so convincingly that it would be difficult to tell if you were communicating with a computer or with a person inputting answers from another room. Design a set of questions that could serve as a test to determine if you are communicating with a machine or a human being.

 CURIOSITY
What would you like to ask a professional mathematician about how the development of the computer has affected his or her work?

 IMAGINATION
Imagine a scenario in which a problem with some newly-developed software leads to a small mathematical error that has devastating consequences for a space travel program.

Simple Arithmetic

Is Arithmetic Simple?

FLUENCY
Make a list of occupations, hobbies, and other daily activities that depend on simple arithmetic.

FLEXIBILITY
Classify the items on your list according to a system of your own design.

ORIGINALITY
Think hard and come up with a way to make learning the multiplication tables enjoyable.

ELABORATION
Expand on your original list of math-dependent activities by making a list of tools and instruments that have been used through the ages to perform operations in arithmetic.

RISK TAKING
Tell how you feel when you are asked—in front of other people—to solve a math problem in your head.

COMPLEXITY
Why is it important to check your answers to arithmetic problems you have solved using only pencil and paper? Is it also important to check answers when you have used a computer or a calculator to solve problems? Explain how checking answers to problems is the same and/or different under these differing circumstances.

CURIOSITY
The branch of mathematics called arithmetic came into being as a result of the curiosity that people have about their lives and their world. Make a list of questions, general as well as specific, that can be answered only through the use of simple arithmetic.

IMAGINATION
Imagine that the use of common fractions and percentages will be declared illegal tomorrow, and that you will be permitted to use decimal fractions alone. Will you be prepared?

Applied Mathematics   **Page 1**
Math: the Language of Science

 ## FLUENCY
Select a field of science in which you have an interest. List all the ways that a knowledge of mathematics is important in this field. As you make your list, consider the ways math is important not only to a professional scientist in your selected field, but to a science student as well.

 ## FLEXIBILITY
Take another look at your list. Find ways to relate the items on your list to other fields of science.

 ## ORIGINALITY
As you work and solve problems in science class, be on the lookout for a time when you make progress in your studies due to an original use of a mathematical concept. This may be a way of using math that has not been defined in your math textbook. These moments of originality sometimes come in a flash! Pay attention when this happens so you can describe this event to someone else.

 ## ELABORATION
Select a difficult problem from your science class that requires the use of mathematics to solve. Rather than concentrating on finding a solution or "the answer" to the problem, focus on the problem itself, relating it to other ideas and concepts, and looking at the reasons for the existence of the problem. It is always a good idea to thoroughly understand a problem before forcing a solution. When you approach a problem this way, a solution may come more easily than usual. You will probably find that this approach to problem-solving is helpful in other fields of study as well as those of math and science.

Math: the Language of Science

RISK TAKING

Tell how you feel about mathematics. Are you more likely to appreciate learning math if you can see there is a practical reason for it? In other words, do you like applied mathematics better than you like pure mathematics?

COMPLEXITY

A school guidance counselor recognizes that a student's interests and aptitudes are very important . . . but this counselor also believes the country has a great need for more fine scientists and mathematicians. Discuss the issues faced by such a guidance counselor who is asked to give career advice to a student who is capable in math and science but who does not particularly enjoy these fields of study.

CURIOSITY

If you could have spoken with Albert Einstein, what questions would you have asked him about his working methods?

IMAGINATION

Imagine you have been hired to tutor a second-grader who is having difficulty with math and who dislikes the subject intensely. Plan your first tutoring session as a presentation intended to spark the student's interest in math. Select an exciting science career in which the student has displayed an interest and show, in detail, how math knowledge is necessary to pursue such a career. Career suggestions: marine biologist, astronaut, explorer, paleontologist.

Using Investigation Cards as an Instructional Tool

Investigation Cards provide a tool for differentiating instruction in a classroom of diverse abilities, interests, and cultures. The cards are designed around Bloom's Taxonomy of Cognitive Development, with three tasks written for each of the six levels. This makes Investigation Cards helpful in "smuggling thinking skills into the curriculum."

Investigation Cards can be used in several ways. Teachers can assign cards to students, or students can select their own cards. Teachers can require students to complete at least one card at each level of the taxonomy, or they can require students to complete cards at any given level or levels of the taxonomy. Teachers can also assign Investigation Cards to cooperative learning groups, with each group having the same set of cards, or each group working on a different set. Finally, Investigation Cards make excellent homework assignments, enrichment assignments, or assignments for students with special needs.

You will need a supply of blank 4" x 6" file cards to prepare the Investigation Cards. Make three copies of each page of graphic cards in this book. Cut apart the cards on the dotted lines and paste each one on the back of one of the 4" x 6" file cards. Then make a copy of each page of task cards, cut apart the cards on the dotted lines, and paste each task card on the back of the appropriate graphic card. If time permits, color the graphics and laminate the set of Investigation Cards for extended use. If time is limited, you may make copies of the task cards alone, cut them apart, and give each student or group of students the paper task cards for immediate use.

Students and teachers can make additional sets of Investigation Cards on topics of their choice by following these simple steps:

1   Select an object or topic of interest to you in your subject area that lends itself to the Investigation Card concept.

2   Collect information associated with your object or topic and use this information to identify major terms, background data, or major concepts related to your Investigation Card theme.

3   Write three different questions, tasks, challenges, or activities for each level of Bloom's Taxonomy using the object or topic as the springboard for ideas. The Bloom Cue Charts found in three Incentive Publications books—*The Definitive Middle School Guide; Tools, Treasures, and Measures;* and *Science Mind Stretchers*—offer excellent guidance for this purpose.

MATH

Investigate a Pair of Dice

GRAPHIC CARD

MATH

Investigate a Pair of Dice

GRAPHIC CARD

MATH

Investigate a Pair of Dice

GRAPHIC CARD

MATH

Investigate a Pair of Dice

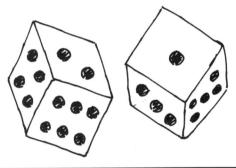

GRAPHIC CARD

MATH

Investigate a Pair of Dice

GRAPHIC CARD

MATH

Investigate a Pair of Dice

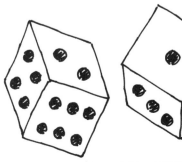

GRAPHIC CARD

KNOWLEDGE

Record the sum total of the number of dots that appear on one pair of dice.

TASK CARD

Investigate a Pair of Dice

COMPREHENSION

Choose a dice game with which you are familiar and explain how the dice are used in the game.

TASK CARD

Investigate a Pair of Dice

KNOWLEDGE

Draw a series of pictures showing the placement of dots on a single die.

TASK CARD

Investigate a Pair of Dice

COMPREHENSION

Describe a pair of dice to someone who has never seen dice or played with them before.

TASK CARD

Investigate a Pair of Dice

KNOWLEDGE

Write down the names of as many card games and board games as you can think of that require a pair of dice.

TASK CARD

Investigate a Pair of Dice

COMPREHENSION

Give examples of how dice could be used in the classroom to teach.

TASK CARD

Investigate a Pair of Dice

APPLICATION

Toss a pair of dice ten times, recording the numbers for each throw. Then toss a pair of dice twenty times, recording the numbers for each throw. Finally, toss a pair of dice thirty times, recording the numbers for each throw. Prepare a summary of your results.

TASK CARD

Investigate a Pair of Dice

ANALYSIS

Determine the types of games that are most likely to be played with dice and the types of games are least likely to be played with dice.

TASK CARD

Investigate a Pair of Dice

APPLICATION

Design a questionnaire to survey others about their favorite games that use dice. Graph your results.

TASK CARD

Investigate a Pair of Dice

ANALYSIS

Deduce how and why you think dice were invented. State your deductions.

TASK CARD

Investigate a Pair of Dice

APPLICATION

Deduce how and why you think dice were invented. State your conclusions.

TASK CARD

Investigate a Pair of Dice

ANALYSIS

Discover ways that dice could be used in subject areas other than math.

TASK CARD

Investigate a Pair of Dice

SYNTHESIS

Invent a game that uses dice.

TASK CARD

Investigate a Pair of Dice

EVALUATION

Defend the use of dice as an instructional tool in the classroom.

TASK CARD

Investigate a Pair of Dice

SYNTHESIS

Write an imaginative story about a "magic pair of dice."

TASK CARD

Investigate a Pair of Dice

EVALUATION

Debate the truth of this statement: **"Throwing dice is both an art and a science."**

TASK CARD

Investigate a Pair of Dice

SYNTHESIS

Create a comic strip that personifies dice. Call the comic strip "The Talking Dice."

TASK CARD

Investigate a Pair of Dice

EVALUATION

Rank the dice games that you know how to play from your least favorite to your favorite. Give reasons for your preferences if you can.

TASK CARD

Investigate a Pair of Dice

MATH

Investigate a Thermometer

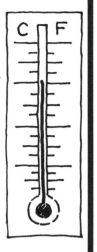

GRAPHIC CARD

MATH

Investigate a Thermometer

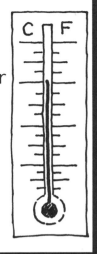

GRAPHIC CARD

MATH

Investigate a Thermometer

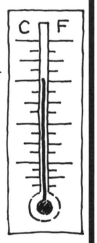

GRAPHIC CARD

MATH

Investigate a Thermometer

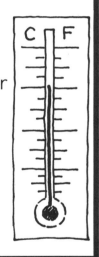

GRAPHIC CARD

MATH

Investigate a Thermometer

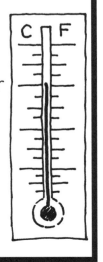

GRAPHIC CARD

MATH

Investigate a Thermometer

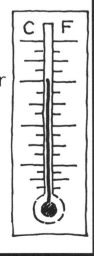

GRAPHIC CARD

KNOWLEDGE

Write down as many words as you can think of using letters from the word THERMOMETER.

TASK CARD

Investigate a Thermometer

COMPREHENSION

Describe the differences between the Celsius and Fahrenheit scales.

TASK CARD

Investigate a Thermometer

KNOWLEDGE

Recall the names of the two types of scales used to indicate temperature change. Draw thermometers to show the increments of each.

TASK CARD

Investigate a Thermometer

COMPREHENSION

Explain how a liquid-in-glass thermometer works.

TASK CARD

Investigate a Thermometer

KNOWLEDGE

List the many uses of a thermometer.

TASK CARD

Investigate a Thermometer

COMPREHENSION

Tell about situations in which it would be appropriate to use a thermometer at home, at school, and in the community.

TASK CARD

Investigate a Thermometer

APPLICATION

Use a thermometer to find differences in temperature of these pairs:

a. water at room temperature and water from the refrigerator
b. closed fist around thermometer and thermometer under armpit
c. soil sample and air samples outside the classroom
d. boiling water and hot tap water

TASK CARD

Investigate a Thermometer

ANALYSIS

Compare and contrast a mercury thermometer with an alcohol thermometer. How are they alike and how are they different?

TASK CARD

Investigate a Thermometer

APPLICATION

Keep track of the temperatures (highs and lows) in your area daily for one week, using both the Fahrenheit and Celsius scales. Chart your findings.

TASK CARD

Investigate a Thermometer

ANALYSIS

Determine what your thermometer is made of and why these materials were used in its manufacture.

TASK CARD

Investigate a Thermometer

APPLICATION

Discuss how the following people might use a thermometer: doctor, chef, meteorologist, scientist, manufacturer, and mother.

TASK CARD

Investigate a Thermometer

ANALYSIS

Draw conclusions about why a doctor uses a mercury thermometer instead of an alcohol thermometer.

TASK CARD

Investigate a Thermometer

SYNTHESIS

Devise ten original real-world math problems involving temperature. Solve the problems.

TASK CARD

Investigate a Thermometer

EVALUATION

Debate the value of using a Celsius thermometer instead of a Fahrenheit thermometer. Justify your opinion.

TASK CARD

Investigate a Thermometer

SYNTHESIS

Compose a diary entry for one day in the life of a thermometer. Use personification to give the thermometer humanlike qualities and experiences.

TASK CARD

Investigate a Thermometer

EVALUATION

Defend or criticize this statement: **"The thermometer has been a minor, not a major, invention in our society."**

TASK CARD

Investigate a Thermometer

SYNTHESIS

Design a new and unusual way to package a thermometer. Draw your package and determine who would be most likely to purchase this product.

TASK CARD

Investigate a Thermometer

EVALUATION

Draw conclusions: Why are so many doctors and hospitals now using digital thermometers with their patients?

TASK CARD

Investigate a Thermometer

MATH

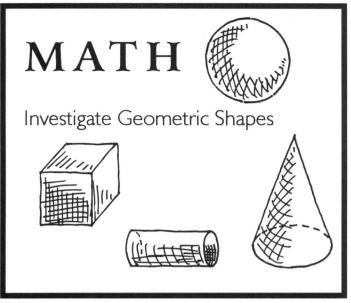

Investigate Geometric Shapes

©1996 Incentive Publications, Inc., Nashville, TN.   GRAPHIC CARD

MATH

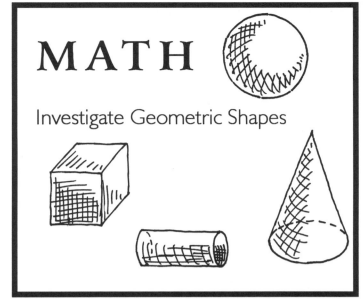

Investigate Geometric Shapes

©1996 Incentive Publications, Inc., Nashville, TN.   GRAPHIC CARD

MATH

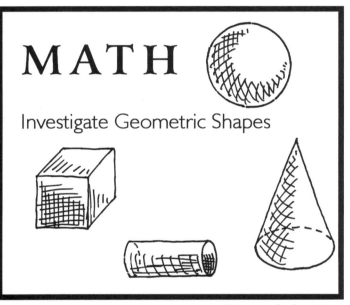

Investigate Geometric Shapes

©1996 Incentive Publications, Inc., Nashville, TN.   GRAPHIC CARD

MATH

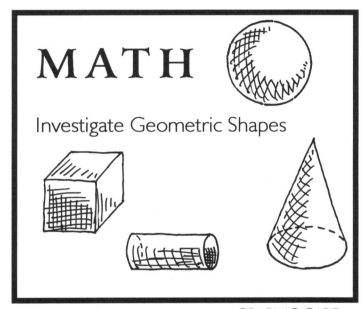

Investigate Geometric Shapes

©1996 Incentive Publications, Inc., Nashville, TN.   GRAPHIC CARD

MATH

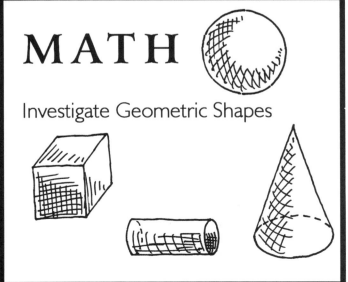

Investigate Geometric Shapes

©1996 Incentive Publications, Inc., Nashville, TN.   GRAPHIC CARD

MATH

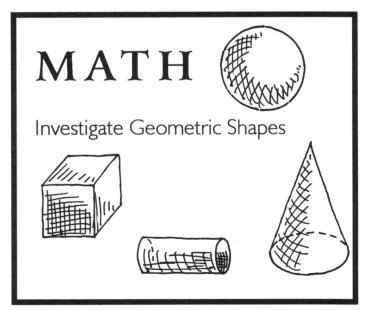
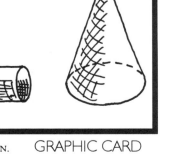

Investigate Geometric Shapes

©1996 Incentive Publications, Inc., Nashville, TN.   GRAPHIC CARD

KNOWLEDGE

List the names of as many geometric shapes as you know. Define each one. Consider both plane and solid geometric shapes.

TASK CARD

Investigate Geometric Shapes

COMPREHENSION

In your own words, explain how you would find the perimeter of a square, the area of a rectangle, the volume of a rectangular prism, and the area of a triangle.

TASK CARD

Investigate Geometric Shapes

KNOWLEDGE

Write the name of one or more geometric shapes you would be able to see in each item in this list. The first one has been done for you.

- glass
  (circle or cylinder)
- shoebox
- ladder
- pair of dice
- table
- coins

- pipe
- sailboat
- bookcase
- checkerboard
- ice cream cone
- book
- crayon

- beads
- eyeglasses
- marbles
- balloon
- telescope
- tray
- pitcher

TASK CARD

Investigate Geometric Shapes

COMPREHENSION

Give examples of geometric shapes found in nature.

TASK CARD

Investigate Geometric Shapes

KNOWLEDGE

Draw each of the following:

a. a pair of similar triangles
b. a pair of parallel lines
c. a pair of perpendicular lines
d. a figure with its line of symmetry
e. a parallelogram
f. an acute angle
g. an obtuse angle
h. a right angle

TASK CARD

Investigate Geometric Shapes

COMPREHENSION

Explain how geometry is used in architecture.

TASK CARD

Investigate Geometric Shapes

APPLICATION

Construct your own model of a cube. Decorate the cube with drawings, illustrations, and words or phrases that reflect the "magical world of shapes."

TASK CARD

Investigate Geometric Shapes

ANALYSIS

Is it important to include geometry in the middle school math program? Draw conclusions and write them down.

TASK CARD

Investigate Geometric Shapes

APPLICATION

Collect pictures from a variety of magazines to show how geometric shapes are found almost everywhere.

TASK CARD

Investigate Geometric Shapes

ANALYSIS

Examine the relationship between geometry and fine art. Mention several periods in art history in which this relationship is quite easy to see.

TASK CARD

Investigate Geometric Shapes

APPLICATION

Make a set of tangrams. Use them to construct a variety of different objects.

TASK CARD

Investigate Geometric Shapes

ANALYSIS

In your opinion, what is most difficult for most students to learn when studying a unit on geometry? Why do you think so?

TASK CARD

Investigate Geometric Shapes

SYNTHESIS

Visualize yourself as a textile designer. Create a series of fabrics using geometric shapes.

TASK CARD

Investigate Geometric Shapes

EVALUATION

Defend or criticize this statement:

"Geometry is a language."

TASK CARD

Investigate Geometric Shapes

SYNTHESIS

Imagine what life would be like if there were no circles. List all of the possible consequences or effects of such a situation.

TASK CARD

Investigate Geometric Shapes

EVALUATION

List all the geometric formulas you know or can locate. Rank them according to order of difficulty for you, with **1** being most difficult. Defend your choices with examples of problems you can and cannot do.

TASK CARD

Investigate Geometric Shapes

SYNTHESIS

Create a "shape" book for a young student to teach him or her about geometry.

TASK CARD

Investigate Geometric Shapes

EVALUATION

If you were going to give the "geometry student award of the year" to someone in your class, who would you give it to and why?

TASK CARD

Investigate Geometric Shapes

MATH

Investigate the
World of Numbers

GRAPHIC CARD

MATH

Investigate the
World of Numbers

GRAPHIC CARD

MATH

Investigate the
World of Numbers

GRAPHIC CARD

MATH

Investigate the
World of Numbers

GRAPHIC CARD

MATH

Investigate the
World of Numbers

GRAPHIC CARD

MATH

Investigate the
World of Numbers

GRAPHIC CARD

KNOWLEDGE

Define these concepts: **whole numbers, odd numbers, even numbers, ordinal numbers, prime numbers, positive numbers, negative numbers,** and **rational numbers.**

　　TASK CARD

Investigate the World of Numbers

COMPREHENSION

In your own words, explain how to add, subtract, multiply, and divide fractions with like denominators and then how to perform these operations with fractions with unlike denominators.

　　TASK CARD

Investigate the World of Numbers

KNOWLEDGE

Record examples from your math textbook of each of these concepts: **whole numbers, odd numbers, even numbers, ordinal numbers, prime numbers, positive numbers, negative numbers,** and **rational numbers.**

　　TASK CARD

Investigate the World of Numbers

COMPREHENSION

Summarize the importance of the location and corresponding value of the decimal point in a variety of situations.

　　TASK CARD

Investigate the World of Numbers

KNOWLEDGE

Recall a school or other real-life situation in which you would need to be familiar with each of these concepts: **whole numbers, odd numbers, even numbers, ordinal numbers, prime numbers, positive numbers, negative numbers,** and **rational numbers.**

　　TASK CARD

Investigate the World of Numbers

COMPREHENSION

Describe the process for changing a decimal number to a percentage and vice versa.

　　TASK CARD

Investigate the World of Numbers

APPLICATION

Develop a set of creative or unusual word problems involving whole numbers for others to solve. Provide an answer key.

TASK CARD

Investigate the World of Numbers

ANALYSIS

Keep records of the most common errors you make in your math computations for a week. Draw conclusions about the nature of these errors and how you might correct them.

TASK CARD

Investigate the World of Numbers

APPLICATION

Compile a mathematical glossary that includes all of the math terms you know and use on a regular basis. Include a definition and a sample application for each one.

TASK CARD

Investigate the World of Numbers

ANALYSIS

Infer what the world would be like without numbers.

TASK CARD

Investigate the World of Numbers

APPLICATION

Collect information about the attitudes of students in your class toward the math topics or concepts that you are studying at the present time. Consider a survey, interview, or questionnaire. Create a graph to show your findings.

TASK CARD

Investigate the World of Numbers

ANALYSIS

Form a set of generalizations about the "wonderful world of zero."

TASK CARD

Investigate the World of Numbers

SYNTHESIS

Design a book jacket for your math text.

TASK CARD

Investigate the World of Numbers

EVALUATION

Compare the study of whole numbers, fractions, decimals, and percentages, and rank them in order of difficulty for you, with **1** being least difficult and **4** being most difficult. Give reasons for your ranking.

TASK CARD

Investigate the World of Numbers

SYNTHESIS

Create a series of informative bookmarks based on a mathematical topic or theme.

TASK CARD

Investigate the World of Numbers

EVALUATION

Imagine there were no fractions. Everything would be all or nothing! Write a paragraph that justifies our need for fractions. Give at least three examples of things we would no longer be able to do if there were no fractions.

TASK CARD

Investigate the World of Numbers

SYNTHESIS

Write an original tongue twister about a math concept.

TASK CARD

Investigate the World of Numbers

EVALUATION

Defend or negate this statement:

"The use of calculators in the math classroom should greatly limit the need we have for learning basic mathematical operations."

TASK CARD

Investigate the World of Numbers

MATH

Investigate Money

GRAPHIC CARD

MATH

Investigate Money

GRAPHIC CARD

MATH

Investigate Money

GRAPHIC CARD

MATH

Investigate Money

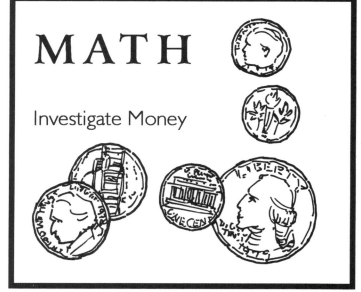

GRAPHIC CARD

MATH

Investigate Money

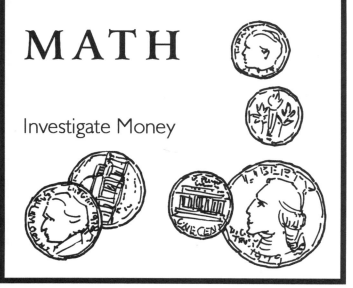

GRAPHIC CARD

MATH

Investigate Money

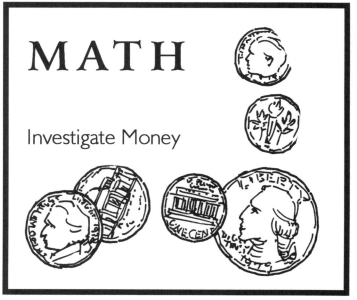

GRAPHIC CARD

KNOWLEDGE

Define these money-related terms:
**monetary, currency, coins, mint,
inflation,** and **barter.**

TASK CARD

Investigate Money

COMPREHENSION

Describe the qualities that forms
of money should have in order
to be convenient to use.

TASK CARD

Investigate Money

KNOWLEDGE

Every country has its own basic
unit of currency. Make a list of
five to ten different countries
and their corresponding units
of currency.

TASK CARD

Investigate Money

COMPREHENSION

In your own words, explain
these three major uses of money:

a. medium of exchange

b. unit of account

c. store of wealth

TASK CARD

Investigate Money

KNOWLEDGE

Make a list of things people in
times past have used as money.

TASK CARD

Investigate Money

COMPREHENSION

Summarize the development of
the first coins and/or the first
paper money.

TASK CARD

Investigate Money

APPLICATION

Construct a flow chart to show how money is manufactured at the United States Mint, where coins are made, and/or the Bureau of Engraving and Printing, where paper money is made.

TASK CARD

Investigate Money

ANALYSIS

Deduce how the expression "two bits" (which means 25 cents) originated.

TASK CARD

Investigate Money

APPLICATION

Construct a timeline to show the history of United States currency.

TASK CARD

Investigate Money

ANALYSIS

Determine how inflation affects the value of money.

TASK CARD

Investigate Money

APPLICATION

Construct a chart to show how the Federal Reserve System adjusts the money supply.

TASK CARD

Investigate Money

ANALYSIS

Infer why all United States currency carries the motto IN GOD WE TRUST and why all United States coins carry the words E PLURIBUS UNUM ("out of many, one").

TASK CARD

Investigate Money

SYNTHESIS

Design a new paper currency and coin monetary system for the United States.

TASK CARD

Investigate Money

EVALUATION

Judge which form of money is most sensible to use for the typical consumer in today's society: checks, credit cards, or cash.

TASK CARD

Investigate Money

SYNTHESIS

Invent a new version of "The Money Game" to teach others more about our monetary system and about the monetary systems of other countries.

TASK CARD

Investigate Money

EVALUATION

Determine the outcome of one of these coin-related experiments in science:

a. If a penny and a dime were left for an hour in the hot sun, which one would feel warmer?

b. If a polished penny were set aside, how long would it take before it turned dark again? Would it happen faster if it were left inside or outside?

c. If a penny were left overnight in a freezer, then dropped on a table, would it make the same sound or a different sound than a dropped penny that had been sitting in the sun?

TASK CARD

Investigate Money

SYNTHESIS

Create a series of original word problems in math that involve money computations.

TASK CARD

Investigate Money

EVALUATION

Decide which one of the following hobbies would be most popular with kids your age and be able to defend your choice:

    a. Collecting coins

    b. Collecting stamps

    c. Collecting baseball cards

    d. Collecting badge buttons

    e. Collecting rocks

TASK CARD

Investigate Money

Using Calendars as an Instructional Tool

Contemporary calendars come in all colors, shapes, and sizes. They cover a wide range of themes and messages, often providing the user with much information for thought and motivation for action. A calendar is considered by many to be an art form and a teaching tool as well as a time management aid. Visit a book store, a gift shop, or the card section of a drug store and you will find calendars for everyone from "cat owners" and "movie buffs" to "Snoopy fans" and "nature lovers." Museums often carry calendars on educational topics.

The calendars on the following pages were designed to be used as mini-interdisciplinary units. The activities were chosen to:

- develop skills;
- introduce new concepts;
- stimulate curiosity; and
- present challenges.

These calendar tasks can be used as:

- enrichment;
- homework;
- extra-credit assignments; or
- an addition to the traditional curriculum.

A wide variety of instructional springboards are included for each day of a typical month. Students can:

- complete each day's task as given;
- select one task to complete each week;
- be assigned a particular set of tasks by the teacher; or
- complete the tasks collaboratively with a group of peers.

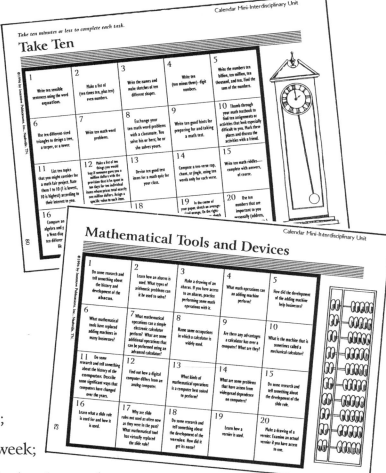

75

One way to introduce the use of calendars as an instructional tool in the classroom is to have students bring in favorite calendars from home or solicit discarded calendars from retail outlets. Display these calendars and use them as the basis for group discussions and/or student observations. Some starter questions or tasks might be:

1 Who would buy this calendar and why?

2 What could one learn by using this calendar?

3 How are graphics, color, layout, and design used to enhance the theme and appeal of this calendar?

4 Why is a calendar considered by some people to be a "form of modern art"?

5 Why would someone want to collect calendars? What could you do with a bunch of old calendars?

6 Research the history of the calendar. Who invented it and for what purpose?

7 If you were going to create an original calendar, what theme or topic would you choose? Develop your idea into a report, a project, or a display with a calendar format.

8 What would life be like without calendars to help us keep track of time, dates, and events?

There's Power in a Math Vocabulary

Read, define, spell, write, and use a word a day to develop a math vocabulary that will serve you well throughout life.

1 Circumference	2 Dodecahedron	3 Polyhedron	4 Trapezoid	5 Hypotenuse
6 Median	7 Quadrilateral	8 Cycloid	9 Octagon	10 Rhombus
11 Equilateral	12 Hexagon	13 Abacus	14 Mean	15 Diameter
16 Parallelogram	17 Tessellation	18 Millimeter	19 Angle	20 Statistics

Develop Your Own Math Power Vocabulary

Find math words in textbooks and other reference materials. Write a word in each calendar space. Exchange completed calendars with a friend, who will learn and use your words as you learn and use his or hers. At the end of the month, each of you has added twice as many new words to your Math Power Vocabulary.

1	2	3	4	5
6	7	8	9	10
11	12	13	14	15
16	17	18	19	20

Math Fun and Games

1	2	3	4	5
Find out what a **magic square** is. Make a 4" x 4" magic square. Turn your magic square into a puzzle.	Design a math wordfind puzzle including at least twenty-two words.	Plan a math party for your class.	Write invitations to the math party in secret code.	Plan your party refreshments (all except the punch) to be served in triangular, circular, square, or rectangular shapes.
6	7	8	9	10
Make up a treasure hunt for the party. All the items to be found should be identified in math terms. *Examples: 1. Find something in the shape of a rectangle. 2. Find something with at least six numbers on it . . .*	Make up a budget for the party. Be sure it is realistic.	Find four round things in the classroom. Measure the circumference of each.	Using the circumference measurements, find the average circumference of the four circles.	Use construction paper, scissors, and paste to form a quadrilateral.
11	12	13	14	15
Create a poster that gives a set of directions for finding palindromes. Include explanations and examples.	Measure your arm from your wrist to your elbow. Measure at least ten objects in your classroom by using your wrist-to-elbow measurement. Determine the most precise measurement possible for each object.	Create a rhyme or mnemonic device to help you remember the order and use of some mathematical process or set of facts.	Estimate the combined age of all the students in your class. Then estimate the average age. Conduct a survey to gather information necessary to find the actual number in both instances. How accurate were your estimates?	Use addition to determine a sum that is a palindrome.
16	17	18	19	20
Determine how much money you would have (in dollars and cents) if you had 996 dollar bills, 20 ten-dollar bills, 35 hundred-dollar bills, 297 half-dollars, 663 quarters, 803 nickels, and 83 pennies.	Predict the average temperature for your locality for the next four days. Check weather reports to test the accuracy of your predictions.	Design a board game based on number combinations. Include rules and scoring procedures.	Create a secret code based on numbers. Use it to send a message to a friend (or maybe to your teacher).	Use any three shapes (as many of each shape as you want) to create an original work of art.

Take ten minutes or less to complete each task.

Take Ten

1 Write ten sensible sentences using the word **equation**.	**2** Make a list of (ten times ten, plus ten) even numbers.	**3** Write the names and make sketches of ten different shapes.	**4** Write ten (ten minus three)- digit numbers.	**5** Write the numbers ten billion, ten million, ten thousand, and ten. Find the sum of the numbers.
6 Use ten different-sized triangles to design a tree, a teepee, or a tower.	**7** Write ten math word problems.	**8** Exchange your ten math word problems with a classmate. You solve his or hers; he or she solves yours.	**9** Write ten good hints for preparing for and taking a math test.	**10** Thumb through your math textbook to find ten assignments or activities that look especially difficult to you. Mark these places and discuss the activities with a friend.
11 List ten topics that you might consider for a math fair project. Rate them 1 to 10 (1 is lowest, 10 is highest) according to their interest to you.	**12** Make a list of ten things you would buy if someone gave you a million dollars with the provision that it be spent in ten days for ten individual items whose prices total exactly one million dollars. Assign a specific value to each item.	**13** Devise ten good test items for a math quiz for your class.	**14** Compose a ten-verse rap, chant, or jingle, using ten words only for each verse.	**15** Write ten math riddles—complete with answers, of course.
16 Compare and contrast algebra and geometry. Use a Venn diagram to show ten differences and/or ten likenesses.	**17** List ten math terms that are important for students of your age to know. Write brief definitions of each of the ten terms.	**18** Draw and label ten different math tools that are used in your school.	**19** In the center of your paper, sketch an average-sized orange. On the right-hand side of the paper, sketch ten round things that are smaller than an orange. On the left-hand side, sketch ten round things that are smaller.	**20** Use ten numbers that are important to you personally (address, phone number, age, etc.) to create a "me" poster.

Math Heroes

Find out the contribution that each of the people in the calendar spaces made (or is making) to the world of mathematics. Learn something about the life and times of each person.

1 Archimedes	2 Fibonacci	3 Sir Isaac Newton	4 Carl F. Gauss	5 The author of your math text (pencil in the name): _____ _____
6 M.C. Escher	7 Euclid	8 Pythagoras	9 Blaise Pascal	10 Benjamin Franklin
11 Max Planck	12 Kurt Godel	13 Bertrand Russell	14 Alfred North Whitehead	15 Lagrange
16 Descartes	17 Nikolai Lobachevsky	18 Albert Einstein	19 Al-Khowarizmi	20 George Boole

Mathematical Tools and Devices

1	2	3	4	5
Do some research and tell something about the history and development of the **abacus.**	Learn how an abacus is used. What types of arithmetic problems can it be used to solve?	Make a drawing of an abacus. If you have access to an abacus, practice performing some math operations with it.	What math operations can an adding machine perform?	How did the development of the adding machine help businesses?
6	7	8	9	10
What mathematical tools have replaced adding machines in many businesses?	What mathematical operations can a simple electronic calculator perform? What are some additional operations that can be performed using an advanced calculator?	Name some occupations in which a calculator is widely used.	Are there any advantages a calculator has over a computer? What are they?	What is the machine that is sometimes called a mechanical calculator?
11	12	13	14	15
Do some research and tell something about the history of the **computer.** Describe some significant ways that computers have changed over the years.	Find out how a digital computer differs from an analog computer.	What kinds of mathematical operations is a computer best suited to perform?	What are some problems that have arisen from widespread dependence on computers?	Do some research and tell something about the development of the slide rule.
16	17	18	19	20
Learn what a slide rule is used for and how it is used.	Why are slide rules not used as often now as they were in the past? What mathematical tool has virtually replaced the slide rule?	Do some research and tell something about the development of the **vernier.** How did it get its name?	Learn how a vernier is used.	Make a drawing of a vernier. Examine an actual vernier if you have access to one.

Using Integrated Instructional Strategies to Promote Cooperative Learning and Group Interaction

Using Cooperative Learning as an Instructional Tool

A cooperative learning group is an excellent means of teaching basic skills or reinforcing important concepts in any content area. Cooperative learning, as described by Johnson and Johnson (1991), involves teamwork within small groups of heterogeneous students working in a structured setting, with assigned roles, and towards a common goal. The five elements that distinguish cooperative learning from traditional group work, according to the Johnsons, are:

POSITIVE INTERDEPENDENCE
. . . requires the students to assist one another in the learning process through common goals, joint rewards, shared resources, and specified role assignments.

FACE-TO-FACE INTERACTION
. . . requires the students to actively engage in discussion, problem solving, decision making, and mutual assignment completion.

INDIVIDUAL ACCOUNTABILITY
. . . requires the student to carry through on "his or her share of the work" and to contribute as an individual to the established common goals.

INTERPERSONAL SKILLS
. . . require group members to learn and apply a range of communication and active learning skills.

GROUP PROCESSING
. . . requires the students to consistently evaluate their ability to function as a group by obtaining legitimate feedback and reinforcement.

Although roles for cooperative learning groups vary, the most common roles are those of Recorder, Time Keeper, Manager, Gopher, and Encourager.

Rules for cooperative learning groups vary too, but the most common are the following:

1 **Students assume responsibility for their own behavior.**

2 **Students are accountable for contributing to the group's work.**

3 **Students are expected to help any group member who needs it.**

4 **Students ask the teacher for help only as a last resort.**

5 **Students may not "put down" or embarrass any group member.**

The size of cooperative groups can range from pairs and trios to larger groups of four to six. It is important to keep in mind, however, that the smaller the group, the more chance there is for active participation and interaction of all group members. Groups of two, for example, can theoretically "have the floor" for fifty percent of the learning time, while groups of five can theoretically do so for only twenty percent of the learning time, if all are to contribute to the group goal in an equitable fashion. Likewise, it is important to note that groups should most often be put together in a random or arbitrary fashion so that the combination of group members varies with each task and so that group members represent a more heterogeneous type of placement. This can be done in a variety of ways ranging from "drawing names out of a hat" to having kids "count off" so those with the same numbers can be grouped together.

There are many different formats that can be used with cooperative learning groups and each of them has its advantages.

On the following pages are descriptions to provide teachers with several structures that can be used in developing lesson plans around the cooperative learning method of instruction. Several applications for each of these structures can be found on pages 89 through 116.

THINK/PAIR/SHARE

In this format, the teacher gives the students a piece of information through a delivery system such as the lecturette, videotape, or transparency talk. The teacher then poses a higher-order question related to the information presented. Students are asked to reflect on the question and write down their responses after appropriate waiting time has passed. Students are then asked to turn to a partner and share responses. Teachers should prepare a plan ahead of time for ways in which students will be paired. If time allows, one pair of students may share ideas with another pair of students, making groups of four. Sufficient time for discussion and for all students to speak should be allowed. The advantages of this structure are:

- It is easy to use in large classes.

- It gives students time to reflect on course content.

- It allows students time to rehearse and embellish information before sharing with a small group or entire class.

- It fosters long-term retention of course content.

THREE-STEP INTERVIEW

In this format, the teacher presents students with information on a given topic or concept. The teacher then pairs students and asks a question about the information such as: "What do you think about . . . ?" or "How would you describe . . . ?" or "Why is this important . . . ?" Each member of the pair responds to the question while the other practices active listening skills, knowing that he or she will have to speak for his or her partner at a later time. Each pair is then grouped with another pair so that each group member becomes one of four members. Person Two answers the question using the words of Person One and Person Three answers the questions using the words of Person Four. Roles are exchanged, and this process is repeated four times. The advantages of this structure are:

- It fosters important listening skills.

- It forces the student to articulate a position or response from another person's perspective.

- It presents multiple interpretations of the same information.

CIRCLE OF KNOWLEDGE

The teacher places students in groups of four to six. A Recorder (who does not participate in the brainstorming because he or she is busy writing down responses) is assigned to each group by the teacher. A question or prompt is given. Everyone takes a turn to brainstorm and respond to the question or prompt, beginning with the person to the left of the Recorder. Responses should be given by individuals around the circle, in sequence, as many times as possible within a five-minute period of time or "until the well runs dry." Group Recorders are asked to report responses from their group to the whole class without repeating an idea already shared by another group Recorder. These collective responses are written on the chalkboard or on a piece of chart paper for all to see.

- This structure is good for review and reinforcement of learned material or for introducing a new unit of study.

- It gives every student an equal opportunity to respond and participate.

- It lets a student know in advance when it is his or her turn to contribute.

- It does not judge the quality of a student's response.

- It fosters listening skills through the rule of "no repetition of the same or similar ideas in either the brainstorming or sharing processes."

TEAM LEARNING

In this cooperative learning format, the teacher places students in groups of four. Each group is given a Recording Sheet and asked to appoint a Recorder and to assign other group roles. The Recording Sheet is a "group worksheet" that contains four to six questions or tasks to be completed. A team must reach consensus on a group response for each question/task only after each member has provided input. The Recorder writes down the consensus response. When the work is finished, all team members review the group responses and sign the Recording Sheet to show they have read it, edited it, and agreed with it. These papers are collected and graded. The advantages of this structure are:

- Students build, criticize (positively), and edit one another's ideas.

- Teachers only have a few papers to grade since there is only one per group rather than one per student.

- Students collaborate on the work for a group grade rather than compete for an individual grade.

A wide variety of springboards can be used for Team Learning questions/tasks such as math manipulatives (tangrams, meter sticks, protractors), reading materials (poems, editorials, short stories), science tools (charts/graphs, rock collections, lab manuals), or social studies aids (globes, maps, compasses).

ROUND TABLE

In this cooperative learning format, the teacher forms groups of four to six members. The teacher gives each group of students a comprehensive problem to solve, an open-ended question to answer, or a complex activity to complete. Each student is asked to consider the assigned tasks and to record an individual response in writing. The key factor is that a group is given only one sheet of paper and one pencil. The sheet of paper is moved to the left around the group and, one at a time, each group member records his or her response on the sheet. No one is allowed to skip a turn. The students then determine an answer to represent the group's thinking, constructing a response that synthesizes many ideas. An optional final stage: each group shares its collective response with the whole class. The advantages of this structure are:

- It requires application of higher-order thinking skills.

- It is useful for reviewing material or practicing a skill.

- It fosters interdependence among group members.

JIGSAW

In this structure, the teacher forms home cooperative learning groups of six members and assigns each member a number from 1 to 6. Each member of a home group leaves that group to join another made up of one member of each of the other groups. The purpose of this arrangement is to have groups of students become experts on one aspect of a problem to be solved or a piece of information to be analyzed. In essence, Jigsaw is so named because it is a strategy in which each member of a given group gets only one piece of the information or problem-solving puzzle at a time. The teacher presents each of the "expert groups" with a portion of a problem or one piece of an information paper to research, study, and acquire in-depth knowledge. Each "expert" member is responsible for mastering the content or concepts and developing a strategy for teaching it to the home team. The "expert" then returns to the home team and teaches all other members about his or her information or problem, and learns the information presented by the other group members as well. The advantages of this structure are:

- It fosters individual accountability through use of the "expert" role.

- It promotes group interdependence through "teaching and learning" processes.

- It encourages the use of high-quality communication skills through the teacher and learner roles.

Student Directions:

THINK/PAIR/SHARE

A **Think/Pair/Share** activity is designed to provide you and a partner with some "food for thought" on a given topic so that you can both write down your ideas and share your responses with each other. Follow these directions when completing the Recording Sheet.

1 Listen carefully to the information on the topic of the day presented by your teacher. Take notes on the important points.

2 Use the Recording Sheet to write down the assigned question or task as well as your response to that question or task.

3 Discuss your ideas with a partner and record something of interest he or she shared.

4 If time permits, you and your partner should share your combined ideas with another pair of students.

5 Determine why "two, three, or four heads are better than one."

A List of Possible
Think/Pair/Share
Springboards for Math

NUMBERS

1. Who invented numbers?

2. Why are numbers important?

3. How do numbers affect our lives?

4. Which is your favorite number? Why?

5. Define counting numbers, rational numbers, and prime numbers.

6. Define composite numbers, even numbers, and odd numbers.

7. How would you explain the concept of infinity to a child?

8. How would you demonstrate the concept of a million of something to a young child?

9. Of what use are squares of numbers and square roots of numbers?

10. Select a topic and use the topic to establish a set, one of its subsets, an intersecting set, and its null set.

11. Discuss the importance of math in the "real world."

12. Explain Base 2 and Base 5.

13. If you were asked to write a numbers autobiography about yourself, which numbers would be included?

14. What does each of these number expressions mean?

    a. She "did a number on him."

    b. "Her number's up!"

BASIC MATH FUNCTIONS

1. Make a list of some common math symbols.

2. Explain what is meant by "borrowing" or "exchanging" during the process of subtraction.

3. Describe how to reduce fractions.

4. What is a repeating decimal?

5. Demonstrate the commutative, associative, and distributive properties of basic math operations.

6. Summarize the process of calculating ratios.

7. Explain ways that percentages are used in sports, in business, or in politics.

8. Discuss how to find averages.

9. Describe the difference between median and mode.

10. What do we mean by rounding off? When is rounding off valuable or even necessary?

11. What are some strategies you use for problem solving?

12. When have you used your estimation skills?

13. How are math signs and symbols important when performing basic math operations?

MEASUREMENT

1. Discuss the advantages of using the metric system over using the English system of measurement.

2. Describe how to find the perimeters and areas of geometric figures.

3. How do you calculate the volume of a container?

4. Discuss the differences between the Fahrenheit and Centigrade scales.

5. Explain military time.

6. How do you change centimeters to meters and feet to inches?

7. Discuss different ways to measure length and distance if a specific measurement tool such as a meter stick or a yardstick is not available.

8. What is the number pi?

9. Discuss measuring situations in which it is important that measurements are precise, and name some situations in which approximate measurements are "good enough."

10. Explain how the development of science has been dependent on the science of measurement.

11. How many dimensions do you think there are, and how can each one be measured?

12. Has it become easier for scientists to make precise measurements? Why or why not?

13. Is there anything that always has precisely the same measurement (such as the temperature of boiling water)?

GEOMETRY

1. What was Pythagoras's great idea?

2. Tell everything you know about points and lines.

3. Explain how to measure angles.

4. When would one want to use a protractor?

5. Describe how geometry is used in art and architecture.

6. What is solid geometry?

7. Discuss the many sizes and shapes of polygons.

8. What makes geometry easy (or hard) to learn?

9. Explain the most common formulas used in geometry to measure perimeter, area, and volume.

10. Create a simple geometric design that could be used as a pattern for a fabric, for wallpaper, or for wrapping paper.

CHARTS AND GRAPHS

1. Explain when it is best to use a bar graph rather than a line graph to convey information. When is it better to use a line graph?

2. Describe a pictograph.

3. Construct a circle graph that tells something important about yourself.

4. Name three important things to remember when constructing a chart or a graph.

5. What is a poll? How are polls a part of our society?

6. Select a social studies topic, a language arts topic, and a science topic. Explain how charts or graphs could aid in the study of each topic.

7. Tell how a chart or a graph could make it easier to solve a difficult math problem.

PROBLEM SOLVING

1. What are some key clue words to look for when solving word problems?

2. Discuss the reasons students may have a difficult time solving word problems.

3. Explain how you solve a word problem in math.

4. Make up four simple word problems. Design each problem so that it is based on one of the four fundamental operations of addition, subtraction, multiplication, and division.

5. Describe a useful problem-solving strategy.

6. Describe the steps that a famous mathematician took in order to solve a famous math problem.

Recording Sheet

Mathematics

NAME_____

DATE_____

QUESTION OR TASK TO BE COMPLETED:

_____
_____
_____
_____
_____
_____
_____
_____
_____

MY IDEAS ON THE TOPIC:

_____
_____
_____
_____
_____
_____
_____
_____
_____

IDEAS SHARED BY MY PARTNER(S):

_____
_____
_____
_____
_____
_____
_____
_____
_____

Student Directions:
THREE-STEP INTERVIEW

In the **Three-step Interview** activity, you will be given some information on a topic by your teacher, then you will work with a partner to discuss your ideas on the topic. You and your partner must take turns as active listener and as active speaker. Follow these directions in order to complete the Recording Sheets.

1 Work with an assigned partner and decide who will be the first speaker and who will be the first listener.

2 Read the information on "The World of Computers" given to you by your teacher. Think carefully about the information.

3 Use the Recording Sheets to prepare your written responses to the five questions. You will use these responses as a basis for discussing the subject with your partner.

4 After talking to your partner while he or she carefully listens to your ideas, exchange roles and let your partner give responses while you listen intently. You may want to take some notes about what he or she tells you.

5 As time permits, you and your partner are to join another pair of students and share opinions and information about the world of computers.

Background Information
The World of Computers

A computer can be compared to a factory. Someone feeds raw material or information through an INPUT device (keyboard). A chip in the computer translates the typed symbols into electrical impulses which travel to the CENTRAL PROCESSING UNIT or CPU, which can be said to play the role of the supervisor of the factory. The CPU sends problems to memory (a gigantic library of "how-to" manuals containing instructions and information). The CPU pulls together instructions on problem solving that are stored in various parts of the memory. The answer to the problem shows up on OUTPUT devices (monitor and/ or printer).

To program means to communicate with a computer in ways that can be understood by the computer. Using a code of letters, numbers, and symbols called a programming language, you can tell the computer what to do and how to do it. The machine changes the letters, numbers, and symbols into electrical impulses— its language.

To write a computer program, a person must organize his or her thinking in order to plan the program in a precise, step-by-step way. Suppose you wanted to make a sandwich. You'd have to figure out exactly how many steps are involved in that activity, and then explain each one clearly. Flow charts are often used for this purpose.

Recording Sheet, Page 1   NAME_____

The World of Computers DATE_____

Use the information on "The World of Computers" to answer these questions and to share with your partner. Be sure to record some of your partner's ideas from the sharing session as well as your own.

1. Create a series of employment ads for outdated math textbooks, classrooms, and teachers who have been replaced by factory-made computers and by computer technology.

YOUR THOUGHTS:

_____
_____
_____
_____

YOUR PARTNER'S THOUGHTS:

_____
_____
_____
_____

2. Write a short, persuasive paragraph explaining why you would rather be taught math by a teacher instead of by a computer.

YOUR THOUGHTS:

_____
_____
_____
_____

YOUR PARTNER'S THOUGHTS:

_____
_____
_____
_____

Recording Sheet, Page 2

The World of Computers

3. Invent a code of letters, numbers, and symbols. Use it to write a message about computers to your partner.

YOUR THOUGHTS:

_____

_____

_____

_____

_____

_____

YOUR PARTNER'S THOUGHTS:

_____

_____

_____

_____

_____

_____

4. Choose a simple task like writing a book report or riding a skateboard and develop a flow chart that communicates step-by-step directions for completing that task.

YOUR THOUGHTS:

_____

_____

_____

_____

YOUR PARTNER'S THOUGHTS:

_____

_____

_____

_____

_____

Recording Sheet, Page 3

The World of Computers

5. Give three reasons that you would or would not like to be a computer scientist.

YOUR THOUGHTS:

_____

_____

_____

_____

_____

_____

YOUR PARTNER'S THOUGHTS:

_____

_____

_____

_____

_____

_____

6. Are you the type of person who loves to learn everything you can about computers, or are you the kind of person who has to be "dragged kicking and screaming into the new world of technology"? Explain.

YOUR THOUGHTS:

_____

_____

_____

_____

_____

YOUR PARTNER'S THOUGHTS:

_____

_____

_____

_____

_____

Student Directions:
CIRCLE OF KNOWLEDGE

A **Circle of Knowledge** activity provides a small group situation for brainstorming responses to a given question or prompt presented by the teacher. Follow these directions in completing the Recording Sheet.

1 Agree on a Recorder for your group. Direct the Recorder to write down the names of all group members and the assigned question or prompt in the appropriate sections of the Recording Sheet.

2 Share your responses to the question or prompt when it is your turn in the circle. Make sure you are ready to respond and that your ideas are recorded as given by the Recorder.

3 Assist the Recorder during the large-group sharing of all responses by helping him or her note which ideas have already been given by the other groups in the class and therefore should not be repeated when it is your group's turn to share.

4 Review the responses generated by both your group and the large group that have been recorded on the chalkboard, transparency, or chart paper.

5 Determine why "two, three, or four heads are better than one."

Recording Sheet

Circle of Knowledge

GROUP MEMBERS:

1. _____
2. _____
3. _____
4. _____
5. _____
6. _____

QUESTION OR PROMPT FOR BRAINSTORMING:

COLLECTIVE RESPONSES:

Sample Questions or Prompts for Circle of Knowledge Activities

MATH

1. Make a list of different units of measure.

2. Think of some numbers that are divisible by 18.

3. List uses of math in everyday life.

4. Make a list of numbers that all contain 3, but in different place values.

5. Think of reasons for kids to learn math in school.

6. List math-related jobs or careers.

7. List some important ways computers have changed our lives.

8. List math terms used when creating and solving word problems (examples: **difference, fewer**).

9. Think of the many things that would result if "money grew on trees."

10. List multiples of 13.

11. Think of things that money can't buy.

12. Make a list of geometric shapes.

13. Write examples of symmetry in nature.

14. List reasons to do your math homework.

15. Make a list of important numbers from history.

16. Think of a number of math-related word games.

17. List types of information that can be appropriately represented by graphs.

18. Name some finite things.

19. Name some infinite things.

20. List ways to spend a million dollars to help people in your school or community.

21. Cite as many mathematical formulas as you can.

22. Name and define math terms.

23. List as many measurement tools as you can.

24. List as many tools for math calculations as you can.

25. Name some famous mathematicians and tell something about each one.

26. Name as many mathematics-dependent tasks you perform in school as you can.

27. Think of the many ways that numbers are used for personal identification purposes (examples: telephone numbers, social security numbers).

28. Write down as many numbers as you can that have been made popular by superstar athletes.

Student Directions:

TEAM LEARNING

During a **Team Learning** activity, your cooperative learning group will respond collectively to questions and tasks. Assign the role of Recorder to one member of your group. The Recorder should follow these directions to complete the Recording Sheet:

1 Assign one of the following jobs to each member of your group so that each person has at least one job: Timekeeper, Coordinator, Checker, and Evaluator (some members may have more than one task to perform).

2 Distribute a copy of the Task Sheet to each group member and a copy of the Recording Sheet plus extra pieces of paper to the Recorder. Ask all to read the questions and tasks.

3 Discuss your ideas for each item and reach consensus on a group response for each item. The Recorder is to write down these collaborative responses to questions and tasks, supplementing the Recording Sheet with additional pieces of paper. The Coordinator is to facilitate the discussion. The Timekeeper is to keep track of the time allotted for the assignment. The Checker is to read through the responses orally, checking for grammar, comprehension, and consensus errors.

4 All cooperative learning group members are to sign their names at the bottom of the Recording Sheet, indicating agreement with the responses and acknowledging fair contributions to the work.

Task Sheet
Math Teamwork

1 Make a list of 50 to 100 different math terms such as **denominator, kilogram, multiple,** and **sum.** On a separate piece of paper, work out a meaningful system of classification for your list of words so that you end up with at least five groups of math terms (though you may have more). Write a paragraph explaining your rationale for each group. As you create your classification system, try to make unusual combinations of math words instead of relying on the obvious.

2 Select any five math words from your list. Make up a three-part riddle for each one, write your riddles on separate sheets of paper, and share them with members of other groups in the class. Start your riddles with this phrase: "I am thinking of a math term that . . ." Here is an example:

I am thinking of a math term that . . .

   a.   is a six-letter word

   b.   describes a system that uses grams to measure weight

   c.   describes a system that measures temperature on the Centigrade scale

(Answer: **metric**)

---

3 On a separate piece of paper, create a crossword puzzle and/or a word find puzzle, using as many words from your list as you can.

4 Stage a "math bee" for members of your group in order to see who can correctly spell each of the words on your list.

Recording Sheet

Math Teamwork

DATE_____

_____

_____
_____
_____
_____
_____
_____
_____
_____
_____
_____
_____
_____
_____
_____
_____
_____
_____
_____
_____
_____

SIGNATURES OF TEAM MEMBERS:

1. _____   4. _____

2. _____   5. _____

3. _____   6. _____

Student Directions:
ROUND TABLE

During the **Round Table** activity, you and your assigned group will examine at least three different math textbooks and record individual responses to a set of questions "round robin" style. The textbooks should cover equivalent areas in the field of math so that you can compare and contrast the presentation and quality of information in each. Follow these directions when completing the Recording Sheets (there will be three sets of each recording sheet).

1 Decide on the order for recording responses. Who will go first, second, third, fourth, fifth, and sixth?

2 Use the Recording Sheets to write everybody's responses to both questions. After the first person writes down his or her idea, the paper is moved to the left around the group. No one may skip a turn.

3 The paper should be passed around the group twice, making certain that each member of the group responds to Question 1 only on the first round and Question 2 only on the second round.

4 One person in the group is responsible for completing information at the top of the Recording Sheet.

5 After both questions have been answered by all six members, the group should analyze the responses and synthesize the ideas into a comprehensive paragraph.

Recording Sheet, Page 1

DATE_____

Math Resources

GROUP MEMBERS:

1. _____
2. _____
3. _____
4. _____
5. _____
6. _____

TITLE OF TEXTBOOK: _____

PUBLISHER AND COPYRIGHT: _____

CHAPTER TOPIC: _____

PAGE NUMBERS: _____

STUDENT ONE RESPONSE

Question 1: What was the strength of this textbook chapter?

STUDENT TWO RESPONSE

Question 1: What was the strength of this textbook chapter?

Recording Sheet, Page 2

STUDENT THREE RESPONSE

Question 1: What was the strength of this textbook chapter?

STUDENT FOUR RESPONSE

Question 1: What was the strength of this textbook chapter?

STUDENT FIVE RESPONSE

Question 1: What was the strength of this textbook chapter?

STUDENT SIX RESPONSE

Question 1: What was the strength of this textbook chapter?

Recording Sheet, Page 3

STUDENT ONE RESPONSE

Question 2: Which illustration/chart/graph/explanation from this textbook chapter was easiest to understand and most helpful to me?

STUDENT TWO RESPONSE

Question 2: Which illustration/chart/graph/explanation from this textbook chapter was easiest to understand and most helpful to me?

STUDENT THREE RESPONSE

Question 2: Which illustration/chart/graph/explanation from this textbook chapter was easiest to understand and most helpful to me?

Recording Sheet, Page 4
STUDENT FOUR RESPONSE

Question 2: Which illustration/chart/graph/explanation from this textbook chapter was easiest to understand and most helpful to me?

STUDENT FIVE RESPONSE

Question 2: Which illustration/chart/graph/explanation from this textbook chapter was easiest to understand and most helpful to me?

STUDENT SIX RESPONSE

Question 2: Which illustration/chart/graph/explanation from this textbook chapter was easiest to understand and most helpful to me?

Student Directions:
JIGSAW ACTIVITY

During the **Jigsaw** activity you will work in a group of six in order to learn something new about lines and angles, and then teach this information to members of your home group. Follow these directions.

1 Assign a number from one through six to each member of your home group. Each student will write down the members of his or her home group on his or her recording sheet.

2 With the help of your teacher, give each member of your group his or her appropriately numbered paragraph describing some important aspect of lines and angles along with a learning task. Don't let anyone see any paragraph but his or her own.

3 When the teacher gives you the signal, locate the other people in small home groups in your classroom who have a number the same as yours. Meet with them and together learn the information discussed in your paragraph so that each of you becomes an "expert" on its content. Work together on the task. You may take notes on the Recording Sheet. The group should then decide on a strategy for teaching what you have learned to the other members of your home group.

4 Return to your home team and teach the information in your paragraph to all of the other team members. Learn the information presented by them in their assigned paragraphs as well.

Recording Sheet

DATE_____

What's My Line and What's Your Angle?

HOME GROUP MEMBERS:

STUDENT 1 _____

STUDENT 2 _____

STUDENT 3 _____

STUDENT 4 _____

STUDENT 5 _____

STUDENT 6 _____

Cut apart the paragraphs about lines and angles. Give each section to the appropriate person in your group. Meet with the other students in the class who have the same number as you do and together learn the information discussed in the paragraph. Work with these same students to complete the follow-up task for your paragraph and share the results with your home group as well.

STUDENT 1   Points and Lines

Points are important in geometry because they tell the positions of lines and objects. Points on a line are labeled with capital letters. Although points have no width, length, or height, they can be used to measure distance and to define the perimeter of shapes and objects. Lines, like points, have no dimensions but they can have infinite length. Points are used to label lines. The line shown below can be represented with this symbol: AB

A   B

TASK: Draw an interesting picture using only points and lines of varying sizes.

STUDENT 2   Parallel, Intersecting, and Perpendicular Lines

Parallel lines are lines that fall within the same plane. They are lines that are always the same distance apart. They never end and they never intersect or touch at any point. Parallel lines are represented by this symbol: ‖
Perpendicular lines are intersecting lines that form right angles.
The symbol for perpendicular lines is: ⊥

AB ‖ CD   EF ⊥ GH

TASK: Think of real-world applications for parallel lines, intersecting lines, and perpendicular lines. When and where are they used?

STUDENT 3   Line Segments and Rays

Line segments are parts of lines and are labeled by two endpoints along the line. They have a specific length and are drawn like this: $\overline{AB}$

A   B

Rays are parts of lines that extend infinitely in one direction. A ray is labeled by its endpoint and one other point: $\overrightarrow{AB}$

The endpoint is always named first.   A   B

TASK: Using your own words, make up a set of True-False statements about rays and line segments that would help other students learn about this topic.

115

STUDENT 4 **Angles**

An angle is formed by two rays with a common endpoint called a **vertex**. An angle is labeled by writing the names of its three points after the symbol for angle or by writing the middle point (the vertex) after the angle symbol. The angle below can be labeled one of these three ways: ∠ZAX ∠XAZ ∠A

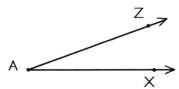

Angles come in all shapes and sizes and are measured with a protractor. Angles are measured in degrees, and they can be any size.

TASK: Find magazine illustrations that show objects that form angles of various degrees. Measure the angles with a protractor.

STUDENT 5 **Acute, Obtuse, Right, and Straight Angles**

Acute angles are angles that measure less than 90 degrees. Obtuse angles are angles that measure more than 90 degrees. Right angles are angles that measure exactly 90 degrees. Straight angles are angles that measure exactly 180 degrees.

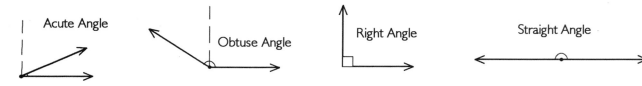

TASK: Tell if each drawn object would form an acute angle, an obtuse angle, a right angle, or a straight angle.

STUDENT 6 **Reflex, Complementary, and Supplementary Angles**

A reflex angle measures more than 180 degrees, but less than 360 degrees (which is a complete circle). Complementary angles form a right angle of 90 degrees when joined together. Supplementary angles form a straight line of 180 degrees when joined together.

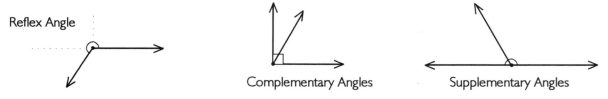

TASK: Create a comic strip or cartoon about reflex, complementary, and/or supplementary angles.

Using Integrated Instructional Strategies to Facilitate Authentic Assessment

An Overview of Authentic Assessment

In comparison with traditional types of assessment, assessment practices today emphasize more authentic ways to demonstrate that student learning has taken place. There is less assessment of the recall of information and more of the processing of information. Collecting evidence about a student over time in realistic settings is the best way to document growth and acquisition of both skills and content.

Product, performance, and portfolio assessment offer alternative assessment methods. They are all more authentic than traditional methods because they:

- require collaboration among student, teacher, and peers;
- encourage student ownership through self-assessment;
- set flexible time limits;
- are scored through multifaceted systems;
- allow for student strengths and weaknesses;
- make use of individual learning styles and interests; and
- minimize competition.

In short, authentic assessment is designed to reflect real-world applications of knowledge whenever possible.

PRODUCT ASSESSMENT
. . . requires the student to produce a concrete end result. This can take many forms, ranging from a videotape or experiment to an exhibit or report.

PERFORMANCE ASSESSMENT
. . . requires the student to actively demonstrate a set of skills and processes while performing a predetermined task.

PORTFOLIO ASSESSMENT
. . . requires the student to maintain a collection of artifacts that reflects the student's overall efforts, progress, and achievements in one or more areas. It is important to note that both products and performances can and should become artifacts contained within the portfolio itself.

Assessment is also made more authentic through the consistent use of rubrics and metacognitive reflections throughout the assessment experience.

Rubrics are checklists that contain sets of criteria for measuring the elements of a product, performance, or portfolio. They can be designed as a qualitative measure (holistic rubric) to gauge overall performance to a prompt, or they can be designed as a quantitative measure (analytic rubric) to award points for each of several elements in a response to a prompt.

Metacognitive reflections are self-assessment observations and statements made by the individual student about each product or performance that he or she has completed. These reflections become part of the portfolio contents.

Although authentic assessment is designed to enhance and support the curriculum rather than dictate or limit the curriculum, it should be noted that more traditional means of measurement such as paper/pencil quizzes, standardized achievement exams, and objective end-of-chapter tests continue to play an important role in today's assessment practices. They should become one type of artifact included in the portfolio or one type of grade assigned to a performance or one type of measure used to determine the value of a product.

Sample Portfolio: Math

My Portfolio Rubric/Conference Questions

RATING SCALE
1 = I could have done better   2 = I did a good job   3 = I did a terrific job

ARTIFACTS

	1	2	3
1. Organization and completeness of portfolio	☐1	☐2	☐3
2. Quality of artifacts selected	☐1	☐2	☐3
3. Creativity shown in work	☐1	☐2	☐3
4. Correctness of work (grammar, spelling, sentence structure, neatness, punctuation, etc.)	☐1	☐2	☐3
5. Evidence of learning concepts and/or applying skills	☐1	☐2	☐3
6. Reflection process	☐1	☐2	☐3
7. Evidence of enthusiasm and interest in assignments	☐1	☐2	☐3
8. Oral presentation of portfolio	☐1	☐2	☐3

QUESTIONS I WISH OTHERS WOULD ASK ME ABOUT MY PORTFOLIO

1. What was your favorite artifact and why?
2. What are the three most interesting math concepts you learned this year?
3. What was your hardest task during this unit of study? What was easiest for you?
4. Would you ever want to be a mathematician? Why?
5. Why is math an important subject?
6. What evidence is there that you have real strength in logical/mathematical intelligence?

GRADING SCALE

22–24 Points = A
18–21 Points = B
14–17 Points = C
10–13 Points = D
Under 10 Points = Unacceptable

My Personal Comments
I enjoyed compiling my math portfolio because it allowed me to select pieces that show all the different kinds of things we learn in math. The most difficult task for me was the measurement drawing. I am good at math, but not so good at art and creative writing. I prefer "hard core" math activities because I am strong in logical/mathematical intelligence.

140   ©1996 by Incentive Publications, Inc., Nashville, TN.

The following pages of this section provide the reader with a sample portfolio in math for a typical middle level student. This prototype is intended to show how authentic assessment—in the form of product, performance, and portfolio samples—can be used effectively to document student growth and achievement over time. It also contains student reflections and self-assessments that are intended to realistically appraise how the student is doing based on his or her own judgment in collaboration with the judgment of others, including the teacher.

Springboards for Journal Writing

REFLECTION STARTER STATEMENTS

1. Something important I learned from today's lesson is . . .
2. A question I have from today's discussion is . . .
3. I would like to know more about . . .
4. An idea from the textbook that puzzles me is . . .
5. I wish I didn't have to remember so much about . . . because . . .
6. I wonder if . . .
7. When I think about the videotape (book, movie), I am surprised that . . .
8. A concept I would like more information on is . . .
9. Some new terms I need to remember are . . .
10. The steps I followed in solving my problem (or completing my assignment) were . . .

SPRINGBOARDS FOR CRITICAL THINKING

1. **HOW ABOUT . . .**

   How about finding out why people like (or do not like) mathematics?

   How about telling us how people use the rules of probability in card games and gambling?

2. **WHAT IF . . .**

   What if we used Base 2 or Base 5 as alternatives to the Base 10 system when learning mathematics?

   What if there were no universal counting or numbering system in our society?

3. **CAN YOU . . .**

   Can you explain what a "googol" is?

   Can you make a list of math skills that everyone should have as a graduating senior in order to be literate in this subject?

4. **WHAT ARE YOUR FEELINGS ABOUT . . .**

   What are your feelings about computers and their impact on your life so far?

   What are your feelings about computers and their potential influence on your life in the future?

SPRINGBOARDS FOR CREATIVE THINKING

1. **YOU ARE AN ADVISOR.**

   What advice would you give a middle school math teacher?

   What advice would you give Pascal about his work with triangles?

2. **YOU ARE AN IMPROVER.**

   How would you improve a meter stick?

   How would you improve our monetary system?

3. **YOU ARE A DESIGNER.**

   Design a protractor that does more than measure angles.

   Design a timepiece that is better than a watch.

4. **YOU ARE A WORD SPECIALIST.**

   Make a list of all the words you can think of to describe a polygon.

   Make a list of all the words you can create by using the letters in the word MATHEMATICS.

5. **YOU ARE A PROBLEM SOLVER.**

   What would you do if you saw someone cheating on a math test?

   What would you do if you met with an adult who didn't know or appreciate anything about computers?

6. **YOU ARE A DISCOVERER.**

   You are a computer buff who just discovered a new piece of very unusual software. Describe what it does.

   You are a mathematician who just discovered a new geometric shape. Draw it.

7. **YOU ARE A WRITER.**

   Write a letter to next year's math students, telling them what to expect in math class.

   Write a thank-you note to Fibonacci, telling him how much you appreciate his work on discovering patterns in nature.

8. **YOU ARE AN IDEA PERSON.**

   Think of ten different uses for a set of pattern blocks, a set of tangrams, or a set of Cuisenaire rods.

   Think of twenty different real-world applications of math concepts.

SPRINGBOARDS BASED ON BLOOM'S TAXONOMY ≣

KNOWLEDGE LEVEL JOURNAL ENTRIES

a. Record the contribution of each of the following ancient cultures to the development of a numbering/counting system: Egyptians, Mayans, Babylonians, Greeks, Hebrews, and Romans.

b. Locate and define five to ten important terms associated with the decimal system.

COMPREHENSION LEVEL JOURNAL ENTRIES

a. Summarize what you know about geometric solids.

b. Give examples of the **commutative, associative**, and **distributive** properties of certain math operations.

APPLICATION LEVEL JOURNAL ENTRIES

a. Discuss reasons that plotting and locating information on a grid are important skills to have.

b. Organize a panel discussion on a mathematics-related topic of your choice. Make a list of important ideas to include in the discussion.

ANALYSIS LEVEL JOURNAL ENTRIES

a. Debate the pros and cons of majoring in mathematics in college.

b. Determine the reasons boys are sometimes thought to be better math students than girls.

SYNTHESIS LEVEL JOURNAL ENTRIES

a. Invent a new numbering system. Write an explanation of it.

b. Imagine you have designed a new math homework machine. Create an ad telling math teachers and students about it.

EVALUATION LEVEL JOURNAL ENTRIES

a. Determine the most difficult topics in math for you to learn and give reasons for your answer.

b. Rank the following mathematical concepts according to the complexity and importance of their function and use in the real world: measurement, fractions, decimals, geometry, probability, graphing, and statistics.

Springboards for Student Products

1. Conduct a survey of student attitudes, feelings, and opinions in your math class, using one or more of the following statements as the basis for your survey. Graph your results.

   - **I like math because I like to solve problems.**

   - **The harder the problems, the better I like them.**

   - **There is more to math than just getting the right answer.**

   - **I think a knowledge of math is useful in everyday living.**

   - **I enjoy mathematics.**

   - **I do not enjoy mathematics.**

2. Prepare a photo essay of geometry in architecture or of symmetry in nature. Organize your photographs (or magazine illustrations, if cameras are not available) in some meaningful way and write a short description of each picture.

3. Create a wrapping paper, fabric, or wallpaper design using a mathematical theme of shapes, numbers, or symbols.

4. Design a series of math-related greeting cards that you could send for birthdays, anniversaries, hospital stays, and special holidays such as Christmas, Valentine's Day, and Halloween.

5. Create a Learning Poster that describes and illustrates all of the many different kinds of math problems that you know how to solve.

6. Research the art of Japanese origami and create a display or exhibit of origami paper folding items. Practice unfolding the objects to examine the varied geometric patterns and shapes created by the different folds. Try to relate these to math concepts such as fractions, sequencing, shapes, and patterns.

7. Write a creative story using one of the following titles or supplying one of your own.

- **The Square Who Wanted to Be a Circle**
- **Life in Absolute Zero**
- **A Day in the Life of a Meter Stick**
- **Numbers Tell It All!**
- **The Math Whiz Kid**
- **The Week That Money Grew on Trees**

8. Invent a series of math games that could be played with a pair of dice, a deck of cards, or a package of play money. Write the directions for your games and teach them to others in the class.

9. Prepare a scrapbook on the different applications and uses of mathematics in the real world. Include an introduction and a conclusion in your scrapbook.

10. Research a number of occupations or careers that require one to have expertise in mathematics. Prepare a Career Fact Sheet for each of these occupations or careers.

11. Create a "how-to" booklet that would teach someone an important math concept or skill. Include explanations, examples, diagrams, and illustrations.

12. Collect a variety of restaurant menus, mail-order catalogs, or store catalogs, and use them to design a set of math problems for others to solve.

13. Create a series of journal entries that might have been written by a famous mathematician.

14. Compile a colorful and interesting dictionary of important mathematical terms. Include math-related jokes, cartoons, riddles, puns, and drawings to make your dictionary more creative.

15. Pretend you are a designer of placemats for a chain of CHILDREN'S LEARNING STORES to be located in shopping malls around the country. It is your job to create a series of placemats displaying mathematical themes such as geometry, metrics, fractions, and whole number operations so that kids can learn as they eat.

Springboards for Performances

1. Organize a "Celebrate Math Week" for your classroom or your school. Prepare and deliver a series of public service announcements and advertisements to promote this event.

2. Locate a poem, essay, picture book, or short story that focuses on a math-related topic or theme. Read it aloud to a group of students.

3. Do some research to find out how numbers and shapes are used in the world of art. Prepare an oral presentation to "share and show" your findings.

4. Prepare a "survival kit" for math students. Demonstrate its contents and respective uses for your classmates.

5. Create and tell a "circle" story that demonstrates some type of life cycle event, circumstance, or experience that has meaning and/or relevance to others.

6. Research the life of a famous mathematician and develop a pictorial timeline to show the important dates and events in his or her life. Use this timeline as an organizing structure for a "chalk talk" you can give to the class.

7. Design a series of mathematical equations that describe special situations, encounters, events, or adventures that have occurred in history such as wars, elections, inventions, or discoveries. Write a detailed description to accompany each of these equations. Present your work with a "transparency talk."

8. Imagine what it would be like to receive the Nobel Prize in Mathematics. Dramatize a dialogue between a recipient of this coveted award and the Nobel Prize Nomination Committee.

9. Conduct a taped interview with someone in your community who has a career in the field of mathematics. Prepare your interview questions ahead of time and use a tape recorder or a videocamera to record the interview process.

10. Develop and deliver an advertising campaign that could be used by a local television station to encourage girls to pursue education and careers in the area of mathematics.

11. Conduct a series of "guided imagery" exercises for learning how to solve word problems in math.

12. Compose and perform a dance, rap, or song that features a mathematical theme such as symmetry in nature, "computer mania," "fraction action," or "wrestle with the decimal."

13. Promote the organization of a math club for your school. Create a math logo, slogan, handshake, set of membership rules, and math-related activities for your club. Plan and deliver a speech to tell others about the plans and benefits of joining this math club venture.

14. Plan and implement a fund-raising project for acquiring additional math resources for your school. Prepare a budget, timeline, and plan of action for this enterprise.

15. Stage a debate that discusses the advantages of the metric system over the English system of measurement. Prepare a series of arguments for and against each type of system.

16. Design a "math calendar" for each month of the school year. Do some research to find interesting events for each day of the month and think of a creative math activity that is related in some way to each event. When a sample monthly page is completed for your calendar, give a "sales pitch" to your teacher, principal, or parent booster club to see if anyone will finance the printing and distribution of this novelty calendar idea.

Examples of Calendar Events/Math Activities for December

December 1: Bingo was invented in 1929. Create a bingo math game.

December 5: Walt Disney's birthday is today; he was born in 1901. Design a new mathematical theme park, Disney style.

December 17: The Wright brothers' flight took place in 1903. Stage a paper airplane contest.

SAMPLE PORTFOLIO FOR MIDDLE GRADES MATH

MY PORTFOLIO:

Interdisciplinary Unit in Math

Puzzles

Number Puzzles That No Longer Puzzle Me

PURPOSE

Number puzzles are often motivating to students because they use numbers in unusual ways to challenge one's thinking and one's perceptions of mathematical concepts. A number puzzle requires a student to use logic to solve a problem.

WHAT I DID

I worked with a friend to collect several number puzzles or brain teasers that we found interesting and that we could figure out in a reasonable period of time. We created a set of "math puzzle cards" with one math puzzle activity per card to challenge other students in the class. Each card had the puzzle on one side and the solution on the other side. Several examples of our "math puzzle cards" are on the next two pages. We put the answers below the puzzles in these examples to save space.

Mean/Median/Mode Tic Tac Toe Game

Define mode.	Explain how to find the **mean** of a set of data.	Describe how to determine the **range** of a set of data.
What is a **median**?	The mean of this set of data is 300. Find the missing number in the data: 300, 320, 280, 360, _____	35, 25, 35, 40, 20, 64, 60, 24, 50 Mode = _____ Median = _____
These are the heights of five members of a basketball team. Which is greater, the median or the mean? 5'6" 6'5" 7'1" 6'2" 5'10"	Six students received the following weekly allowances: $15.00 $10.00 $8.00 $20.00 $5.00 $10.00 Range = _____ Mode = _____ Median = _____	Summarize how averages, means, and medians are used in probability and/or statistics.

Reflection:

This activity was nice because I could work with a friend and because I could spend some math time working on number puzzles instead of doing worksheets and textbook assignments. One of my favorite paper-and-pencil games is Tic Tac Toe. I made a bunch of Tic Tac Toe worksheets to use as study guides for tests. Each worksheet features a common math concept. The problem in the middle cell is always the hardest one to solve. A sample Tic Tac Toe worksheet is shown on the left.

SAMPLE

MATH PUZZLE CARDS

FROM

MY COLLECTION

CARD **1**

Using each number only once, fill in the circles with the numbers 1, 2, 3, 4, 5, 6, and 7 so that each row of three circles adds up to 12.

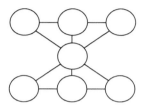

ANSWER:

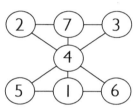

CARD **2**

Place ten coins on the table in a triangle like this:

By moving only three coins, can you make the triangle point down instead of up?

ANSWER:

CARD **3**

$$23 + 9 = 32$$

See how the digits of the number 23 are reversed when you add 9. To which other two-figured numbers can you add 9 in order to reverse their digits?

ANSWER:

12, 34, 45, 67, 78, 89

MORE

SAMPLE

MATH PUZZLE CARDS

FROM

MY COLLECTION

CARD **4**

How many triangles can be found in this large triangle?

Without lifting your pencil, draw 4 straight lines through these dots. Every dot should be passed through at least once by a line OR should provide a place where two or more lines meet.

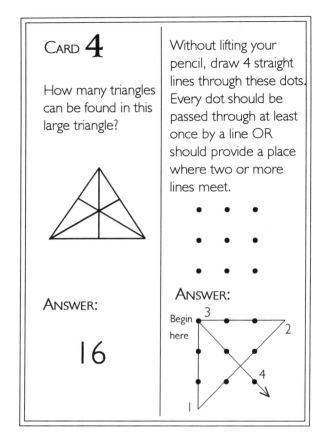

ANSWER:

16

ANSWER:

CARD **5**

Can you make this problem correct?

1 2 3 4 5 6 7 8 9 = 100

Use any of the signs +, -, x, and ÷ between the numbers to the left of the equal sign, or move two numbers together to form one single-digit number as necessary.

ANSWERS:

1 - 2 - 3 + (4 X 5) + 67 + 8 + 9 = 100

1 + (2 x 3) + 4 + 5 + 67 + 8 + 9 = 100

(-1 + 2) x (34 + 56 - 7 + 8 + 9) = 100

and more

CARD **6**

Using only four straight lines, can you cut an octagon into five geometrical shapes—a triangle, two rectangles, a parallelogram, and two trapezoids?

ANSWER:

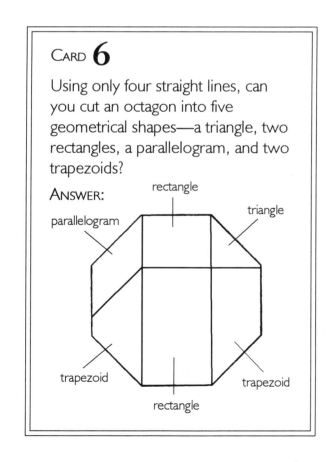

130

Candy Makes Math
Sweeter to Swallow

PURPOSE

Many math concepts and skills can be practiced or learned through the use of manipulatives—even when the manipulatives are candies! "Learning by doing" makes math easier to understand because you can actually "see" and "feel" the solutions to math questions and problems. Small candies are best for this purpose. BEWARE: Students may eat the manipulatives!

WHAT I DID

For this activity, I used the following materials:

- Package of small, round plain chocolate candies
- Package of small, soft gumdrops
- Package of jellybeans

All of the packages weighed the same, although the number of candies in each package varied.

I completed the following tasks:

1. I estimated the number of candies in each package.

2. I counted the number of candies in each package to check my estimate.

3. I separated the candies from each bag into separate colors and tallied the number of candies of each color.

4. I used the totals of each color to make three different bar graphs, one for each type of candy.

5. I wrote fractions to represent the ratios of the different colors to the total number of candies for each type of candy.

6. I drew three king-sized geometric shapes (triangle, square, circle) on a large piece of drawing paper and estimated the number of each type of candy that would cover the areas of these figures. I checked my estimates.

7. I used the three types of candies to create an interesting series of color patterns.

Reflection

This activity was one of my favorites because it was fun, interesting, and helped me understand mean, median, and mode. I was very good at the estimation part of this activity and my color pattern was so attractive that I made it into a drawing for my portfolio. My bar graphs are part of my portfolio file.

Creating a

Measurement Drawing

PURPOSE

Drawing is a science as well as an art. When figures and objects in a picture must be drawn in proportion to one another, the artist uses measurement so things can be drawn to scale. Drawing a picture is an art partly because one must be creative in deciding what to draw and how to represent it. Drawing original pictures according to a given set of measurement specifications can be both a challenge and a pleasure.

WHAT I DID

Our science teacher gave us directions for creating an original drawing related to our study of weather concepts. We were instructed to use a set of English measurement specifications for some of the objects in the picture. We could add other things to the drawing, but could not omit any of the required "specs." I drew a picture of a summer storm in our rural community. It included the following measurement specs.

1. Draw a thunderhead cloud between 5 and 6 inches in length and between 2 and 3 inches in height.

2. Draw a tree $9^3/_4$ inches high that has a trunk 1 inch wide.

3. Draw a bird flying $1^1/_4$ inches above the top of the tree.

4. Draw a building that is $3^1/_8$ inches taller than the tree.

5. Draw an inanimate object 1 inch in diameter.

6. Draw three triangles, each with each side no longer than 1 inch.

7. Draw two items that have 2 $^1/_2$ inches between them.

Reflection

I didn't like the way my picture turned out because things were either too big or too small for the drawing space I had. It's hard to create a picture when there are so many precise measurements and shapes that must be included. My teacher suggested I redraw the picture using measurements and shapes of my own choosing. I did that. When I compared the results, I realized I liked the first drawing better after all.

Learning Log

Inventory of Math Skills

PURPOSE

Our teacher encourages us to keep a learning log of math skills which we have studied and can perform with a high degree of accuracy. Although not all these skills were taught this year in class, many of those learned in earlier years were relearned and reinforced when we worked problems in our math textbook.

WHAT I DID

I reviewed my learning log and made a list or inventory of all the different things I know how to do in math. These are:

WHOLE NUMBERS
- Adding and carrying numbers
- Subtracting and borrowing from numbers
- Multiplying and dividing numbers
- Rounding off numbers
- Estimating numbers
- Recognizing rational numbers, prime numbers, composite numbers, even numbers, odd numbers, and square roots of numbers
- Applying commutative, associative, and distributive properties of math operations
- Finding averages, modes, and medians of numbers
- Recognizing place values of numbers

GRAPHS
- Making a grid
- Plotting and locating information on a grid
- Constructing bar graphs, line graphs, circle graphs, and pictographs

FRACTIONS
- Changing improper fractions to proper fractions
- Finding common denominators
- Finding least common multiples
- Changing mixed fractions to improper fractions and vice versa
- Adding and subtracting fractions
- Recognizing equivalent fractions
- Multiplying, inverting, and dividing fractions
- Changing a fraction to a decimal

DECIMALS
- Recognizing decimal fractions and decimal numbers
- Recognizing decimals and their place values
- Changing a decimal to a fraction
- Working with repeating decimals
- Working with decimal/fraction equivalents
- Adding and subtracting decimals
- Multiplying and dividing decimals
- Calculating ratios and percentages

MEASUREMENT

- Measuring length and distance using both English and metric systems
- Measuring weight using both English and metric systems
- Measuring perimeter and area
- Measuring volume
- Measuring temperature
- Measuring time
- Converting metric measures to English measures and vice versa

GEOMETRY

- Recognizing and working with geometric concepts of: points, lines, line segments, rays, parallel lines, intersecting lines, perpendicular lines, planes, angles, polygons, triangles, quadrilaterals, and circles
- Working with the Pythagorean Theorem
- Working with symmetry, congruence, and similarity
- Measuring angles with protractor
- Drawing circles with compass

MISCELLANEOUS

- Working with powers and exponents, including palindromes
- Solving word problems and writing equations from story problems
- Learning the language of statistics
- Solving problems with calculators
- Investigating the language of probability
- Working with computer simulations

Reflection

Reviewing the entries in my learning log and reading through my math textbook/notebook helped me realize how much I have learned in math this year and in previous years. I like math and math comes easily to me, except for ratios, percentages, and statistics. I love number puzzles and challenges. We could do these activities for extra credit. I think I want to be a math teacher when I grow up.

Our Study of Animals
My Word Problems

PURPOSE

Word problems involving mathematical operations can often be designed around studies in science or social studies. Solving and creating such word problems help students see relationships between math and other curriculum areas. It is a good teaching strategy to have students create original word problems for themselves as well as for others to solve.

WHAT I DID

The teacher assigned our cooperative learning group the task of reviewing several pages of word problems from our math textbook. We were instructed to look for "clue words" in each problem. These clue words help us decide which operation(s) to use in order to find a solutions to the problem. We developed a list of clue words for addition, subtraction, multiplication, and division problems. We used these clue words to help us create a series of word problems around facts we learned about animals during our recent study of mammals in science. We wrote the problems and provided an answer key for the solutions. Several of our word problems were given to other students as homework assignments. My word problems, along with an answer key, are in my portfolio file.

SOLVING MATHEMATICAL WORD PROBLEMS FOR OUR STUDY OF ANIMAL LIFE IN SCIENCE

The following clue words will help me solve word problems more effectively:

ADDITION CLUE WORDS	SUBTRACTION CUE WORDS	MULTIPLICATION CLUE WORDS	DIVISION CLUE WORDS
add	subtract	times	quotient of
sum	difference	product of	divided by half (or by another fraction)
total	take away	multiplied by	
plus	less than	by	as much
in all	are not	how many	split
both	remain	how much	separated
together	decreased by		cut up
all together	have left		parts
increased by	how much more		sharing something equally
	fewer		

These are my original word problems about animals based on facts I found in my research:

FACT 1 *The white-tailed jackrabbit can run as fast as 45 mph.*

PROBLEM 1 How far might a jackrabbit run in 12 hours if it could run as fast as possible without stopping? How far in 24 hours?

FACT 2 *A lion sleeps up to 20 hours per day.*

PROBLEM 2 If a lion slept its daily maximum for a total of 1860 hours, how many days would that be?

FACT 3 *An elephant spends 23 hours a day eating.*

PROBLEM 3 How many hours during a year would a herd of 37 elephants spend eating?

FACT 4 *An adult porcupine has about 30,000 quills.*

PROBLEM 4 How many porcupines would there most likely be in a group if one counted a total of 840,00 quills?

FACT 5 *A camel drinks up to 22 gallons of water at a time.*

PROBLEM 5 How many quarts of water could 67 camels possibly drink at one time?

FACT 6 *Blue whales weigh 7 tons at birth.*

PROBLEM 6 What is the combined weight of 14 newborn baby whales?

Reflection

I don't mind working word problems if they aren't too hard and if they are about subjects that interest me. I think it is hard, however, to make up good word problems that are fair and that make sense to the reader. It is easier to solve word problems than to create them. In order to create one, you first have to collect factual information about the subject.

Two Reviews of
Picture Books about Mathematics

TITLE:
The Greedy Triangle
AUTHOR:
Marilyn Burns
ILLUSTRATOR:
Gordon Silveria
PUBLISHER:
Scholastic, 1994

This is a witty story about a triangle who wanted to be a different shape because it was tired of having only three sides and three angles. Even though the Greedy Triangle supported bridges, made music in symphony orchestras, and caught wind for sailboats, it wanted to be a quadrilateral.

Greedy Triangle approached the shapeshifter many times to try life as a pentagon, a hexagon, and many other geometric figures, only to discover that it had acquired so many sides and angles that it couldn't tell which side was up!

The Greedy Triangle finally decided to get its own shape back because life was really more fun when one could become slices of pie, halves of sandwiches, and the shape of things when people put their hands on their hips.

This book has an appendix which provides the reader, parents, teachers, and other adults with information about mathematics and with extension activities for stimulating children's thinking about shapes.

TITLE:
**The Librarian Who
Measured the Earth**
AUTHOR:
Kathryn Lasky
ILLUSTRATOR:
Kevin Hawkes
PUBLISHER:
Little, Brown, and Co., 1994

The story of this picture book takes place more than two thousand years ago, when a very smart baby named Eratosthenes was born to a family in ancient Greece. Eratosthenes was a curious child who was always asking questions about the world around him.

He had one burning question, however, that no one could answer, which was: "How can I measure the earth without walking around the world?" He knew that the earth was round, but he wanted to know how big around it was.

Eratosthenes was able to develop a formula of numbers that measured the earth so accurately that it was only two hundred miles different from our own scientific calculations of today.

Reflection

This was one of my favorite activities because it was easy and fun to do. I was amazed to find out how much one could learn from a book written for young children. Two other picture books I strongly recommend are: *I Spy Two Eyes,* by Lucy Micklethwait, published by Greenwillow Books of New York in 1991 (a book about numbers in art); and *The King's Commissioners,* by Aileen Friedman, illustrated by Susan Guevara, published by Scholastic in 1994 (a book about various ways to count).

My Number Report on Mexico

PURPOSE

Numbers can provide organizational structures for papers in subjects other than mathematics. Numbers should also be used as a source of information when preparing reports.

WHAT I DID

I used numbers to structure a report on Mexico for social studies. I did some research on Mexico and then organized my facts around the counting numbers one through ten (1–10). This helped me share a lot of ideas in a readable form.

I included the following in my report:

 **10** Ten important numbers in the demographics and geography of Mexico, including areas, populations, heights of mountains, lengths of rivers and lakes, and coastlines.

9 Nine key dates in Mexico's modern history, beginning with 1808 when Mexico fought for independence from Spain and ending with 1988 when Hurricane Gilbert wrecked Cancun, an island resort in Quintana Roo.

8 Eight interesting words and/or phrases in Spanish, the national language of Mexico.

7 Seven special festivals or fiestas that honor patron saints of the church or national holidays that celebrate heroes such as Benito Juarez, President of Mexico in 1858.

6 Six key facts about the country's capital, Mexico City, the world's most crowded and fastest-growing city.

 **5** Five famous tourist attractions, including two volcanoes, the Great Desert, the Sierra Madre mountain range, and the Copper Canyon Railway.

 **4** Four Mexican foods popular with local populations *and* with tourists, including tortillas, mole poblano, chile con carne, and quesadillas.

 **3** Three cultural events, including mariachi bands made of trumpeters, guitarists, violinists, and a singer; mural wall paintings in Mayan temples; and the charreada, the Mexican version of the rodeo.

 **2** Two serious problems facing the Mexican people: overpopulation and devaluation of the Mexican peso.

1 One significant observation about Mexico: its reputation as a country of beautiful contrasts.

Reflection

I enjoyed this assignment because I am going to visit Mexico next summer with my parents. Now I know what I want to see and do in this fascinating country. Since Mexico is a neighbor of ours, I think it is important to understand its people and policies. The numbering system helped me organize my data.

My Portfolio Rubric/Conference Questions

RATING SCALE

1 = I could have done better   2 = I did a good job   3 = I did a terrific job

ARTIFACTS

1. Organization and completeness of portfolio   ☐ 1   ☐ 2   ☐ 3
2. Quality of artifacts selected   ☐ 1   ☐ 2   ☐ 3
3. Creativity shown in work   ☐ 1   ☐ 2   ☐ 3
4. Correctness of work (grammar, spelling, sentence structure, neatness, punctuation, etc.)   ☐ 1   ☐ 2   ☐ 3
5. Evidence of learning concepts and/or applying skills   ☐ 1   ☐ 2   ☐ 3
6. Reflection process   ☐ 1   ☐ 2   ☐ 3
7. Evidence of enthusiasm and interest in assignments   ☐ 1   ☐ 2   ☐ 3
8. Oral presentation of portfolio   ☐ 1   ☐ 2   ☐ 3

QUESTIONS I WISH OTHERS WOULD ASK ME ABOUT MY PORTFOLIO

1. What was your favorite artifact and why?
2. What are the three most interesting math concepts you learned this year?
3. What was your hardest task during this unit of study? What was easiest for you?
4. Would you ever want to be a mathematician? Why?
5. Why is math an important subject?
6. What evidence is there that you have real strength in logical/mathematical intelligence?

GRADING SCALE

22–24 Points = A

18–21 Points = B

14–17 Points = C

10–13 Points = D

Under 10 Points = Unacceptable

My Personal Comments

I enjoyed compiling my math portfolio because it allowed me to select pieces that show all the different kinds of things we learn in math. The most difficult task for me was the measurement drawing. I am good at math, but not so good at art and creative writing. I prefer "hard core" math activities because I am strong in logical/mathematical intelligence.

A Very Practical Appendix

Student Activities to Integrate Instruction through Planning and Carrying out a Math Fair

1. Determine the main objectives of the math fair, and record the objectives for class use.

2. Recruit volunteers (teachers and parents) who have good organizational skills and an interest in math to serve on the math fair committee.

3. Set a time, location, and date for the math fair.

4. Arrange for schedule, space, and total school involvement with the proper administrative staff.

5. Write the math fair rules. Include such things as the entry deadline, size limits for displays, requirements for final reports and logs of observations, the completion deadline, judging guidelines, and awards.

6. Compile a list of suggested math fair topics.

7. Design an entry form. Include a place for the student's name, project title, hypothesis, method, materials, and student and parent signatures.

8. Draft a cover letter (to be endorsed by the principal) which introduces the fair and explains the rules.

9. Design the evaluative criteria and a corresponding evaluation form. Include charts, graphs, and other appropriate measurement devices.

10. Publicize the application deadline, the date of the math fair, and the awards.

11. Prepare posters and bulletin board displays to be placed in the halls, the cafeteria, and in other common areas in order to generate interest throughout the school.

12. Contact and secure judges.

13. Plan the math fair layout. Draw a floor plan for efficiency.

14. Plan, type, and reproduce the math fair program.

15. Send each judge a judging packet which includes the fair rules, the judging criteria, and a list of the projects to be judged in his or her area of expertise. Arrange to meet with the entire judging panel if possible.

16. Order or make certificates, ranging from entry-level certificates to prize-level certificates, all explained in the evaluative criteria.

17. Gather the necessary materials and equipment such as tables, chairs, and a portable address system.

18. Send thank-yous to parent and teacher volunteers, judges, and demonstrators after the math fair.

Ten High-interest Strategies/Activities to Integrate Social Studies into Math

1 **Use Venn diagrams to compare and contrast people, places, events.**

Example: Compare and contrast the New England colonies of Massachusetts (Plymouth), Rhode Island (Providence), and Connecticut (Hartford), using the following variables: year founded, founder, chief crops of trade, government, and religion.

2 **Construct line graphs, bar graphs, circle graphs, and pictographs.**

Example: Construct a line graph to show the immigration pattern for Florida during the last ten years.

3 **Create word or story problems.**

Example: Did you know that 20 to 50 inches of dry, powdery snow when melted yields just one inch of water? How much snow in the coldest parts of Russia would be needed to generate 12 inches of water according to this formula?

4 **Use money and monetary systems of the United States and other countries.**

Example: Using a currency conversion chart from your local newspaper, convert $10.00 in U.S. dollars to the foreign currency in dollars for Japan, France, and Mexico. Which country would give you the greatest value if you were to visit that country on a vacation?

5 **Construct flow charts or diagrams to show processes for making or doing something.**

Example: Construct a diagram to show how a bill becomes a law.

6 **Discover the elements of geometry in different cultures by examining art, architecture, monuments, artifacts, homes, and lifestyles.**

Example: Do some research to find out the role that geometry played in the construction of the Pyramids of Egypt, the Great Wall of China, the Eiffel Tower of Paris, and the Golden Gate Bridge of San Francisco.

7 **Conduct individual or group surveys and show results in chart form.**

Example: Take a survey of the students in your class to determine their ancestries. Show your results in chart form.

8 **Use number codes or ancient number systems to rewrite math problems or social studies facts.**

Example: Use a number code to write three key facts about the American Revolution. See if a friend can decipher your code and uncover your facts.

Example: Use the number symbols of the Egyptians to rewrite one of your math problems from today's math class.

9 **Construct timelines to establish the chronology of important events.**

Example: Make a timeline to show the most significant events in the life of a famous explorer, inventor, or political leader.

10 **Use linear measures to determine distances on a map.**

Example: Use the mileage scale on a U.S. map to determine the best route to take when driving from Detroit, Michigan, to Toronto, Canada.

Ten High-interest Strategies/Activities to Integrate Science into Math

1 **Use the scientific method to test a hypothesis.**

Example: Create a hypothesis as a base of inquiry to determine why boys tend to do better in mathematics classes or courses than do girls during the middle grade and/or high school years.

2 **Identify cause and effect situations.**

Example: Examine the use of the metric system in your science textbook and give reasons why the study of metrics in mathematics may be very important to you.

3 **Construct a flow chart or diagram to show a process for making or doing something.**

Example: Construct a flow chart to show the process for solving word problems in addition, subtraction, multiplication, and division of fractions.

4 **Discover the role of elements of science in different mathematical content areas.**

Example: Use the Beaufort Wind Scale and the Fahrenheit thermometer to measure the wind speed and temperature in your community every day for a week. Display these measurements in chart form.

5 **Brainstorm to generate lists of information.**

Example: Look through your science book and write down as many uses of mathematical formulas and computations as you can find. Use these to develop a list of ways to integrate math concepts into science class.

6 **Look for patterns and repetitive designs.**

Example: Do some research to explain the numbering system used in the Periodic Table of Elements.

7 Use manipulatives to demonstrate applications of science concepts.

Example: Use a variety of measurement tools to measure the volume, mass, and temperature of different states of matter.

8 Use scientific laws or principles to perform mathematical operations.

Example: Use Ohm's Law to measure the force of electricity.

9 Use concept webs to explain mathematical ideas.

Example: Draw a concept web to show the connections between symmetry and/or geometry and nature.

10 Use scientific observations to study real-world applications of mathematics.

Example: Visit a local supermarket or department store and observe how math skills are used daily in the operations of the business. Record your observations in a Learning Log or Journal.

Ten High-interest Strategies/Activities to Integrate Language Arts into Math

1   **Write reports or speeches and give them orally.**

Example: Prepare a short "speech to inform" that explains how geometry is used in architecture or how geometry is used in bridge construction.

2   **Express information through various forms of poetry.**

Example: Use appropriate poetry forms such as concrete poems, acrostic poems, free verse poems, diamante poems, or couplets to describe various polygons.

3   **Use diaries or learning logs to record feelings, ideas, reflections, and observations.**

Example: Keep a diary to record your experiences with the computer and its many different types of software.

Example: Maintain a learning log in which you collect examples of various charts and graphs from magazines and newspapers. Paste them in your log and summarize the information you learned from each one.

4   **Use children's literature and picture books.**

Example: Collect a series of picture books about mathematics. Read the books and write a synopsis for each one. Determine what makes these books both appealing and informative.

5   **Read folktales, legends, myths, and tall tales.**

Example: Look for the use of numbers and mathematical concepts in the folklore that you read.

Example: Invent a mythological goddess of numbers or a folktale character only five centimeters tall and write about your protagonist's adventures on Mount Olympus or in the Magical Kingdom of Mathematics.

6   **Use reference resources such as the dictionary, *Guiness Book of World Records*, or *Bartlett's Familiar Quotations* as tools to acquire information or conduct research.**

Example: Use the dictionary to define these terms related to our study of statistics: range, median, mode, and mean.

Example: Use *The Guiness Book of World Records* to locate interesting mathematical facts, figures, and records that pertain to a particular theme. Graph or chart your findings.

Example: Use *Bartlett's Familiar Quotations* to locate quotations related to various areas of mathematics and/or learning.

7 Write and send friendly or business letters.

Example: Follow news of the stock exchange and investing reports in your local newspaper. Write to one of the companies listed on the New York Stock Exchange to inquire about the value of the company's stock.

8 Read biographies of famous mathematicians.

Example: Develop an outline of information about a mathematician whose biography you chose to read. Use this outline to share information about the mathematician with members of your math class.

9 Compose original short stories.

Example: Choose one of the following topics about which to write an original story related to our study of measurement:

- **Pi is Not for Dessert**
- **The Weight We Were**
- **Brrrrrr! Absolute Zero**
- **The Forgotten Timepiece**
- **The Ruler That Wouldn't Measure**

10 Incorporate grammar into tasks.

Example: Make a list of common nouns, proper nouns, adjectives, or verbs that best describe the properties of numbers or the use of fractions or the phenomena of optical illusions.

Example: Stage a "spelling bee" in which the words to be spelled are mathematical terms, formulas, and concepts.

Example: Browse through your textbook or a popular magazine and select a picture that shows a topic or situation that is related to mathematics in some way. Use the picture as a springboard for a declarative sentence, an interrogative sentence, an exclamatory sentence, and a sentence that gives a command, all related to the mathematical content of the illustration.

Topics for Student Reports

NUMBERS AND NUMBER SYSTEMS

All about Sets

Arabic Numbers

Base 2

Base 5

Digits to Base 10

Even and Odd Numbers

Fibonacci Numbers

Googol

Infinity

Large Numbers: a Billion Plus

Palindromes

Perfect Numbers

Prime Numbers

Rational Numbers

Rectangular Numbers

Roman Numerals

Sequences and Series

Sets

Squares and Square Roots

Tally Systems

Triangular Numbers

Whole Numbers

Zero

BASIC MATH FUNCTIONS

Babylonian Fractions

Clue Words in Story Problems

Fractions, Proper and Improper

Integers

Inverting Fractions

Math Symbols

Means, Medians, Modes

Order of Operations

Properties: Commutative, Associative, and Distributive

Repeating Decimals

Rounding Off

Strategies for Solving Word Problems

Zero in Multiplication

GEOMETRY

Circles

Objects in Three Dimensions

Pythagoras's Great Idea

Quadrilaterals

Regular Solids

Symmetry, Congruence, and Similarity

Topology

MEASUREMENT

Absolute Zero

Ancient Calendars

Calculating Areas

Calculating Volumes

The Centigrade Scale

Clocks of the _____ Century

Daylight Saving Time

The Fahrenheit Scale

History of Measurement

The Importance of Pi

Leap Day, Leap Year

Military Time

Nanoseconds

Nautical Measurement

Space Age Measurement

Vectors

Why Pound is Abbreviated "lb."

RATIOS

Scale Drawing

Special Ratios

DISPLAYING DATA

Bar Graphs

Circle Graphs

Histograms

Linear Graphs

Nonlinear Graphs

Spreadsheets

FAMOUS MATHEMATICIANS

Albert Einstein

M.C. Escher

Euclid

Sir Isaac Newton

OTHER TOPICS

Abacus

Discount Percentages

The First Calculators

Fractals

Monetary Systems

Probability and Statistics in Action

Software and Hardware

Interdisciplinary Unit in Math

Title: _____

Topic (or Theme): _____

Purpose

Objectives

Glossary

Introductory Activity

Activities or Projects in Related Content Areas

SOCIAL STUDIES

SCIENCE

LANGUAGE ARTS

ENRICHMENT OR EXPLORATORY

Homework or Independent Study Projects

Cooperative Learning Activity

Culminating Activity

Assessment

Integrating Math to Accommodate Multiple Intelligences

Math Theme: _____

	Social Studies	Science	Language Arts
VERBAL/ LINGUISTIC			
LOGICAL/ MATHEMATICAL			
VISUAL/SPATIAL			
BODY/ KINESTHETIC			
MUSICAL/ RHYTHMICAL			
INTERPERSONAL			
INTRAPERSONAL			

NOTE: Not every square need be filled in for every topic. Just make sure there is a good content balance in each unit.

Integrating Math to Accommodate Williams' Taxonomy

Math Theme: _____

	Social Studies	Science	Language Arts
FLUENCY			
FLEXIBILITY			
ORIGINALITY			
ELABORATION			
RISK TAKING			
COMPLEXITY			
CURIOSITY			
IMAGINATION			

NOTE: Not every square need be filled in for every topic. Just make sure there is a good content balance in each unit.

Teacher Checklist to Aid in the Promotion of Journal Writing in the Math Classroom

Purposes

How do you present the purposes of a journal to your students when you are making journal assignments?

A journal is a . . .

a. ____ sourcebook/collection of ideas, thoughts, and opinions.

b. ____ place to write first drafts/ outlines of papers and projects.

c. ____ place to record observations of and/or questions about something read, written, or discussed.

d. ____ recordkeeping tool to use to keep track of what and how much was read/researched on a topic.

e. ____ place in which to write personal reactions or responses to a textbook assignment, group discussion, research finding, or audiovisual resource.

f. ____ reference file to help a student monitor individual growth or progress in a given area.

g. ____ way for students to "dialogue" in written form with peers and teachers.

h. ____ place for a student to write about topics that he or she has chosen.

i. ____ place for reflections on and paraphrases of material learned.

Formats

Which of the following journal formats is most appealing to you?

a. ____ special notebooks

b. ____ segments of audiotapes

c. ____ file cards

d. ____ handmade diaries

Writing Time

Which of the following time options is most practical for you?

a. ____ daily for five minutes

b. ____ semi-weekly for ten minutes

c. ____ weekly for fifteen minutes

d. ____ when needed

Student Feedback

Which of these formal/informal methods makes most sense to you?

a. ____ student sharing of journal entries with peers

b. ____ reading journal entries aloud to class on a volunteer basis

c. ____ using journals for "conferencing"

d. ____ taking journal entries home to share with parents/guardians

e. ____ analyzing and answering one's own journal entry one or more days after entry was recorded to acknowledge personal changes in perspective

Annotated Bibliography

An annotated bibliography of Incentive Publications titles selected to provide additional help for integrating instruction in math

Breeden, Terri and Kathryn Dillard. *The Middle School Mathematician: Activities That Lead to Success in Algebra and Geometry.* **Nashville, TN: Incentive Publications, 1996.** *(Grades 5–8)*

These challenging activities in the areas of rational numbers, algebra, and geometry were created to reflect the changing math curriculum, which places less emphasis on basic skill drills and more emphasis on technology and problem-solving strategies.

Forte, Imogene and Sandra Schurr. *Making Portfolios, Products, and Performances Meaningful and Manageable for Students and Teachers.* **Nashville, TN: Incentive Publications, 1995.** *(Grades 4–8)*

Filled with valuable information and specific suggestions for incorporating authentic assessment techniques that help students enjoy a more active role in the evaluation process. Includes a convenient pullout Graphic Organizer with creative ideas for integrating content instruction and appraising student understanding.

—. *The Definitive Middle School Guide: a Handbook for Success.* **Nashville, TN: Incentive Publications, 1994.** *(Grades 5–8)*

This comprehensive, research-based guide is a perfect overview for educators and administrators. Includes nuts and bolts of middle grades education, interdisciplinary teaming, advisory, cooperative learning, creative and critical thinking skills, assessment, and interdisciplinary instruction.

—. *Tools, Treasures, and Measures for Middle Grade Success.* **Nashville, TN: Incentive Publications, 1994.** *(Grades 5–8)*

This practical resource offers a wide assortment of teaching essentials, from ready-to-use lesson plans and student assignments to valuable lists and assessment tools.

Frender, Gloria. *Learning to Learn.* **Nashville, TN: Incentive Publications, 1990.** *(All grades)*

Comprehensive learning resource is filled with creative ideas, practical suggestions, and "hands on" materials to help students acquire the organizational, study, test-taking, and problem-solving skills they need to become lifelong effective learners.

Annotated Bibliography

Frank, Marjorie. *Kids' Stuff Book of Math for the Middle Grades.* **Nashville, TN: Incentive Publications, 1988.** *(Grades 4-7)*

Creative, stimulating math activities stretch reasoning abilities as well as teach number concepts, addition and subtraction, multiplication and division, fractions and decimals, geometry, problem solving, measurement, time and money, and more.

Frank, Marjorie. *Math Bulletin Boards.* **Nashville, TN: Incentive Publications, 1986.** *(Grades K–6)*

Each bulletin board was designed to build specific math skills through suggested activities and visual stimulation. Includes clear instructions for assembly and use plus suggestions for activity extensions.

Math YELLOW PAGES for Students and Teachers. **Nashville, TN: Incentive Publications, 1988.** *(Grades 2–8)*

Skills checklists, math properties, formulas, tables, processes, symbols and meanings, a complete glossary of math terms, shortcuts, math "tricks"—these are just some of the useful and timesaving lists in this book.

Opie, Brenda, Lory Jackson, and Douglas McAvinn. *Masterminds Addition, Subtraction, Place Value, and Other Numeration Systems.* **Nashville, TN: Incentive Publications, 1994.** *(Grades 3–7)*

Jumbo-sized collection of thematic-based interdisciplinary activities and assignments created to spark interest, encourage communication, and promote problem solving as well as decision making.

Opie, Brenda, Lori Jackson, and Douglas McAvinn. *Masterminds Decimals, Percentages, Metric System, and Consumer Math.* **Nashville, TN: Incentive Publications, 1994.** *(Grades 4–8)*

Students can practice reading and writing decimal notation, determining place value in decimals, comparing and rounding numbers, finding percentages, and using metric units . . . and have fun at the same time!

Opie, Brenda, Lory Jackson, and Douglas McAvinn. *Masterminds Fractions, Ratio, Probability, and Standard Measurement.* **Nashville, TN: Incentive Publications, 1994.** *(Grades 3–7)*

Students working these fun-filled assignments will find least common multiples and greatest common denominators, identify prime and composite numbers, use factor trees, find equivalent fractions, reduce to lowest terms, change fractions to whole or mixed numbers, and perform computations involving fractions and mixed numbers.

Index

Index entries in bold type are titles of student activities.